GET RID OF
YOUR BULLSHIT
LIFE
AND KICK ASS

GET RID OF
YOUR BULLSHIT
LIFE
AND KICK ASS
HOW TO WIN IN LIFE

TANIA DAMHA

Maktub
LOS ANGELES

© 2020 by Tania Damha
Published by Maktub

*All rights reserved. Printed in the
United States of America.*

This book may not be reproduced in whole or in part, in any form or by any means, electronic or mechanical, including photocopying, recording, or by any information storage and retrieval system now known or hereafter invented, without written permission from the publisher.

Maktub Books may be purchased at special discounts for bulk purchases in the United States by corporations, institutions, and other organizations. For more information, please contact us at Maktub by emailing info@taniadamha.com.

Designed by Euan Monaghan

First Edition

ISBN 978-1-7352122-0-3

Los Angeles

Visit Tania on the web!
www.taniadamha.com

CONTENTS

Introduction 1

PART 1: GET YOUR ACT BACK

Chapter 1: Brutally Honest 11
Chapter 2: Resistance 22
Chapter 3: Marathons and Volcanoes 37
Chapter 4: Eating Habits 52
Chapter 5: Better Your Thinking 60
Chapter 6: No Debt 79
Chapter 7: Release Your Anger 89

PART 2: HOW TO LIVE BULLSHIT-FREE

Chapter 8: More Time in Nature 99
Chapter 9: Solo Travel 106
Chapter 10: Focus Is Your Best Friend 117
Chapter 11: Burn Your Ships 127
Chapter 12: Feel Fear and Still Go for It 135
Chapter 13: Saying No 145
Chapter 14: Accept Setbacks 152

PART 3: DEVELOP AN EXCELLENT LIFE

Chapter 15: Forgiveness 165
Chapter 16: Giving 171
Chapter 17: Acceptance 180
Chapter 18: More Time Alone 188
Chapter 19: Reading Books................................. 195
Chapter 20: Creating Communities 206
Chapter 21: Sex Transmutation or Less Sex 216
Chapter 22: Discipline..222

PART 4: LIVE AN INTENTIONAL LIFE

Chapter 23: Friendships......................................229
Chapter 24: Gratitude...236
Chapter 25: Power...243
Chapter 26: Resourcefulness 251
Chapter 27: Consistency of Habits..................... 257
Chapter 28: Positive Mindset..............................266
Chapter 29: Love...272
Chapter 30: Why Not?..283

Acknowledgments... 291

INTRODUCTION

NEVER MEASURE THE HEIGHT OF A MOUNTAIN UNTIL YOU HAVE REACHED THE TOP. THEN YOU WILL SEE HOW LOW IT WAS.
—Dag Hammarskjöld

Suddenly a birthday threatened to turn me, a highly energetic spring chicken, into a lifeless bear. I was far removed from my ideal life. "You are going to be F-O-R-T-Y, and your life is still a mess!" I warned myself. I was not prepared. I was a real adult now; I needed to become serious and stop dreaming so much. I needed to get my act together.

I wish this book existed when I needed it most. I was lost, craving romantic love, lonely, and still searching for my life's purpose. The truth was right in front of me—a provoking mirror I couldn't look away from. Specific issues were holding me back from the success I wanted. I had made mistakes, some necessary and some unnecessary, because I had not discovered the right tools to live a satisfying life yet. I felt like a huge failure. I read a lot of books, but none gave me the honest and practical advice that I desperately craved. I needed to make some big changes but did not know how, because I was stuck. That's why I wrote this book. I wanted to get out of this nightmare.

I was desperately waiting for a wakeup call. At the time, I believed my life was over, but, to my surprise, I found out that life was just beginning. When I faced that mirror and was brutally honest with myself—taking a hard look at what I needed to change—I realized I had the liberty to determine who I wanted to be and what my life was about. I went through a process to achieve success on my terms. I discovered feeling like a failure wasn't that bad. I could change and get rid of this inadequate feeling.

I am still in process, but we all are. Right?

If you're feeling like your life is over, or your best years are behind you, or you can't achieve success at your age, I'm here to tell you those are lies you are telling yourself. I went through a process to achieve success, and I want to show you how I did it.

> Whether you're turning thirty or sixty, you can push beyond your boundaries and find that your best years are still ahead of you.

Rediscovering Your Dream

I was an idealist and still am, but my worries shook my faith temporarily. "Maybe I should become wiser and stop being such a big dreamer," I thought.

I had done risky things in life—quitting a corporate job during a thriving finance career and buying a one-way ticket to Los Angeles to fulfill my Hollywood dream as an actress, as well as starting companies as an entrepreneur—but I still wasn't where I wanted to be. I was unimpressed with myself. When I took these risks, some people thought I was crazy to let go of a prestigious job and forgo a great future, just for silly dreams, and I thought they were crazy to stay. I didn't want to be stuck for the rest of my life selling checking accounts and writing letters to people who had overdrawn ten bucks on their account.

I wanted an electrifying life. I wanted to see the world, meet exciting people, and not be chained to a nine-to-five job with only a few weeks of vacation per year. I craved to hear my heartbeat explode from all the excitement I encountered daily. I aspired to leave my footprints all over the world and create meaning for others. If you're reading this book, you most likely want to change too but do not know how. What was I going to do? Despair and waste more years, or become super clear on how to proceed? When I was younger I did not fully commit to my goals, and now I wish I had. You may be in the same boat. I want to help you rediscover your dreams or create new ones and get rid of that horrible sense of failure.

> I want you to get rid of the bullshit and kick ass, like your life depends on it, because it does!

Find Your True Calling

I struggled many years until I found my true calling. I was always passionate about writing but did not have the balls to go for it.

"Become serious, Tania!" "Get a regular job." "Why can't you be like your friends?" "That ideal life you desire isn't worth the risks."

The voice in my head repeated many crappy thoughts. I heard it thousands of times and acted like a sheep for years. But deep in my heart grew a seed I had nourished. It blossomed, and in hindsight, I am glad I did not listen to my destructive voice. I woke up from stagnation. I stopped delaying and creating the wrong kind of outcomes and living the wrong life. I aligned with my destiny and committed. No matter what would happen, I would go for it and stop wasting time. I took a leap of faith and let go of my timid tendencies, so I could accomplish my destiny. I gave myself permission to change.

Meanwhile, the world was moving forward without delays. I got an important call. My sister called me up and told me she was pregnant. I was happy for her, but at the same time also thought, "She is creating life. What the fuck are you creating, Tania?"

It Was Then That I Saw the Light

I decided to listen to myself and be completely honest about what I wanted. I would not become a mom like her, but I could give birth to my book and bring joy, clarity, and meaning to others. I decided to let go of everything that was not supporting my goals. I realized that I could do the impossible. I recognized the lies I told myself about not being able to live my dreams. I stopped fabricating piles of excuses that instilled fear and caused wasted years.

> I finally became my own hero, and this gave me confidence.

Perhaps you have an unfinished project that's important to you, or you've put aside a passion of yours for various reasons. Work, family, responsibilities, they're all important. But you're important too. You may think you don't have the time or have other priorities. But if you don't do it now, later in life you may regret it.

And regret is a bitch.

The journey I have taken led me to drop all the bullshit in my life and find clarity. It showed me what I wanted in my life. It saved my life.

> See this book as a tool to save you from falling off a cliff called "wasting your life."

The Decision to Follow the Heart

I want to help you follow your heart and finally do what you love. I will teach you how to change forever and go after the life you always wanted. When I reevaluated my life, I confronted many things that needed attention, which you'll read about in the following thirty chapters.

It's time to create your own revolution and go after the life you always wanted. You will see the untruths you told yourself about why you could not succeed. You will get rid of the bullshit and push yourself forward. It is important not to let more years go to waste.

> The future is bright. Do what you love.
> Your life depends on it.

Believe in yourself, especially in the darkest moments. One of those defining moments for me was when I stared at my bank account, as an adult woman, close to her forties, and saw only thirty-three cents, with weeks before another paycheck would arrive. I had a breakdown and did not understand why I was not succeeding. Would I be eighty years old and still be poor? Hell no! I needed to stop feeling like a failure.

> I had had enough of my current situation. It made me sick to my stomach.
>
> I had done cool stuff in the past, but it wasn't till I did what I wrote in this book that my life changed.

You can find your success, too, even if you feel like you missed the boat. Reach your wildest dreams and keep them! Let fear disappear, and skyrocket into a bullshit-free and kick-ass life.

My wish is to erase the fear you may have about "doing" what needs to be done. Turn your life around and be a contender. Win in life, because you've committed to doing what needs to be done. Let's lock our fears in a museum and watch them behind glass coverings. Fear does not direct our lives anymore. You kicked that piece of sh*t out!

> Your life is just beginning!

PART 1
GET YOUR ACT BACK

CHAPTER 1:

BRUTALLY HONEST

AND THE POINT IS, TO LIVE EVERYTHING.
—Rainer Maria Rilke

You have to be brutally honest.

Please read this sentence again, slowly: You have to be brutally honest. What is keeping you from living your ideal life? For some it is fear, for many it is pleasing others, and for others it is a lack of clarity. To find out what you need to overcome to progress fruitfully, you must search within yourself first and be brutally honest.

Before Clarity Came to Me

One evening I cried and cried till I had no tears left. I looked around at my green walls, the same damn green walls my ex-husband painted a decade ago, a clear signifier of me not changing, and did not understand why I was still stuck in a little studio on Hollywood Boulevard after seventeen years. Why did I stay in a place that felt like a prison? I thought I could not make enough money to move to a better place. I had the best intentions about moving but lacked the radical willpower to do it. I was scared as hell.

I understood other areas that needed improvement and change, but the alteration was always a short-term one. Instead, I found myself only numbing my pain: "That delicious ice cream shop around the corner will take my sorrows away." I ran to consume the different sugary flavors, which would heal me temporarily, instead of signing up for CrossFit. I did not keep my full attention on my intentions. I briefly changed, but it was always superficial.

I also did not change my habits. I was living in a city where dreams were made every single day, but those dreams were still far away for me. I saw the famous Hollywood sign from my apartment every morning. Every day I was reminded of the success stories this city brought to the lucky ones—yet I was not one of the lucky ones yet.

....

I was unhappily sunk in a denying state of mind.
I had to be completely honest with myself.

I knew deep inside that I was not reaching
high enough. My low rent was my heroin.

....

I was content with my situation because I did not feel the urgent need to change. Would I stay trapped in a place that killed my dreams and made me unhappy, or would I take a risk? Would I take a chance even if this change was scary, unfamiliar, and could potentially be a wrong decision? It came down to being brave enough to tell myself that my underwhelming life was *not* my destiny. My fear was burying my real wishes. I wanted to become the me that I would be proud of. My still-to-be-awakened potential self needed to go onto high rooftops and yell: "I am more than I am living! Wake up! Stop wasting away your precious life!"

Why was I not doing things differently? I had to go through long teary nights with swollen eyes to come up with effective conclusions. My new me had to be reborn, and only if I faced fear head-on and confronted my issues would I move and live more happily.

....
Brutal honesty is your rescuer, and it comes down to getting rid of one fundamental cruel thought we have: that we are not able to do it.
....

We tell ourselves lies like, "I can't do this," "I am not beautiful enough," or "It's too late since I'm a certain age." We hear so many can'ts that we stay put and live life in fear. We keep digging our graves instead of finding our ideal paradise that was always out there waiting to be reclaimed, but we were just too blind to see it. Our eyes are closed.

> Let us open our eyes widely, beat out accumulated fear once and for all and live that amazing life we desire—a life we only have one of in this world.

Get That Humongous Microscope Out!

Think about looking at your life under a gigantic microscope. What do you see? Take a moment to reflect on everything under the glass. Write down the things you want to change. *Be honest.* There will be no permanent and positive change if you deceive yourself. Lying is easy, and the truth is hard to swallow sometimes.

Carve out some alone time to analyze yourself, and then create a blueprint that will help you reclaim your life. What do you need to change? Look at your finances, love life, eating habits, relationships, jobs, health, exercise, what you do in your leisure time, and the way you think and behave.

Write down specific issues that are holding you back. Be brutally honest about what you want and what you need to do to get what you desire.

A Bitter Pill Called *Existential Angst*

In my thirty-nineth year, something switched inside of me. Until that age, I was convinced that I was only getting younger. I did not believe that I would grow older. What a bunch of BS. I had the energy of a thirteen-year-old and thought that society made up this thing called *aging*. I was not going to comply, but an unpleasant feeling grew inside of me that would not go away. This particular anxiety has a name: *existential angst*. It is a realization that life lacks meaning, causing an extreme form of anxiety and a feeling of despair and hopelessness.

Existential angst makes you aware of your upcoming death, for you are the one responsible for your life. You make decisions and live with the consequences. You are the painter and choose your colors and tools. Do you use a bright or a dark palette? Are you a modernist or more impressionistic? How will you create a portrait of your life? It's yours, and yours alone.

We Are What We Decide to Be

In this existential state, we become aware that everything is in our hands. It feels liberating at first but then becomes a burden. You are running out of time. The hourglass is upside down, losing its sand, slipping away fast. The end is closer. What do you do? Do you despair? Or do you find a solution that leads you to an authentic life? I thought life was endless before the crisis hit me, and I began to understand and feel the boundaries of my existence. I knew I had to change, but did not know how, so I decided to write a letter to my future eighty-year-old self. I hoped that looking into the future would give me wisdom on what to do in the present.

This is the letter I wrote:

Los Angeles, August 22, 2012

A letter to my eighty-year-old self

Forty years ago, you came across a major crossroads in your life. You chose not to stop. You chose to continue your journey despite all the major obstacles, like tiredness, shame, being broke, feeling stuck, feeling lonely, and a big unknown future ahead of you. You came home from a long walk and realized that fearlessness, freedom, and fun should be your constant mantras. Do not deviate from your path. All the years you struggled had a purpose. They made you strong. I am not giving up now. Not after you survived so many hurdles.

You are resilient. You are nature. Be like nature.

That day you realized more than anything that you have to conquer yourself. The wise men from the past were right. Plato said it wisely, "The first and greatest victory is to conquer yourself." Conquer thyself. That is what needs to happen. First conquer yourself, and then create beauty. It is that simple, but why is being simple so hard? It doesn't have to be. You made a pact with yourself to shed your fear, anger, and limitations and start anew, fresh like a bright new morning.

You continued your path, a road you paved because you believed in something bigger and more powerful than yourself. You wanted to let everything out that was inside of you and share it with others.

> I am so grateful that I found that life sparkle and nurtured its life force so that I could become the person I was meant to be.

End of letter

Write Your Own Letter to Your Eighty-Year-Old Self

Writing this letter was a springboard to changing my life. When you look back on your life and write from that perspective you get a deeper clarity and take the action needed to change. Write your own letter to your future eighty-year-old self.

Find an inspiring place, sit down, get a cup of coffee or tea, and relax into your body. Then write this important letter. Imagine that you are eighty years now and are looking back on your life. Tell yourself that you did not give up in difficult times, when younger, which made all the difference. This letter is very powerful. It is time to be brutally honest and ask deep questions.

The poet Rainer Maria Rilke advises us to "live [our] questions now." He wrote, "Don't search for the answers, which could not be given to you now because you would not be able to live them. And the point is, to live everything. Live the questions now. Perhaps then, someday far in the future, you will gradually, without even noticing it, live your way into the answer."

Find those important questions, and they will lead you toward your freedom. We gain advantages through wisdom, and hopefully feel more peace of mind, so take life by the horns and roar like a lion. Become that lion. I am here to help you. Roar!

Oh, the Excuses We Make

There is a quote by Winston Churchill: "If you're going through hell, keep going." It is applicable when wanting to make lifelong changes. You will find the truth if you are willing to embrace pain so it can transform you into a healthier place.

It is difficult to be brutally honest. It seems impossible at times, but it is possible, and that is what counts. We humans do not want to be honest. We like to run away from our pain because we'd rather indulge in endless pleasures. We come up with certain thoughts that are temporary Band-Aids for our wounds. "Oh, that person does not like me? That's because they have issues." "Oh, my boss does not want to give me a raise? That's because he favors other coworkers." "Oh, my sister is not calling me? That's because she is prioritizing her business instead of wanting a healthy relationship with me." "Oh, that dress doesn't fit anymore? That's because it is the holidays. I should be eating and not thinking about portion control. On January 1st I will start dieting again." But real change always happens in the now.

One of my favorite philosophers, Krishnamurti, said, "Change is instant. Otherwise it is just a modification."

> Brutal honesty is your main objective, so you can get rid of feeling like a failure.

Recurring Thoughts That Should Be Banned

Analyze thoughts that are not helping you. What thoughts do you repeat day in and out that are destructive instead of empowering? Why do you keep telling them to yourself? Do they give you false comfort, so you do not have to change? Those restrictive thoughts need to go. Send them out to distant lands on a giant vessel.

Unfortunately, negative thoughts are often automatic. They become a habit. When you deconstruct limiting recurring thoughts, you will be able to change them. Give yourself some slack. Habits are not easy to change. Acknowledge faulty thoughts, and then change them into positive affirmations. Do a rewrite inside your brain.

For example, I never thought I would enjoy exercising. I was wrong. Now I love it. I rewired my limiting beliefs around working out into empowering thoughts. I see myself running, checking my heartbeat on my watch, seeing my body become healthier and stronger. It is a transformation I never thought would happen, because I was thinking wrong before. I now love my toned leg muscles.

> You are what you decide to keep thinking about.

Self-Analysis Is Your Savior

Self-analysis in the moment is a powerful tool. I was able to self-analyze myself on a Sunday evening when I overate again. While reading a book about habits, I rushed to eat some nougat I had kept in my cabinet for three months. I was explicitly reading this book to get rid of my bad habit of eating too many candies. How sad to read a book on changing habits, but instead of following the advice, eating old nougat instead!

What happened during my self-analysis?

Transform Anger into Understanding

Instead of getting angry about what I had done, which often causes more overeating, I analyzed my behavior like a detective. At the time, I wasn't hungry. I had eaten a bag of salty snacks before eating the nougat. What had triggered this irrational eating? In the moment, I had opposing thoughts that made me panic. I thought that I should eat the nougat early because when I finished reading the book about habits, I was going to be a changed woman! Hallelujah! I had rewarded myself for the anticipated change already, but this change had not occurred yet. It is like going shopping with a credit card with no money in the bank. You anticipate making money, so it's okay to shop with plastic. "I better eat it *now*," I thought. My reward system was faulty. I should have put in the work first.

My other thought was that I might not want it after reading the book, and *that* would be a tremendous waste of a delicacy. I had a case of FOMO (fear of missing out), so I acted irrationally again. Those opposing thoughts created chaos and made me over-eat.

I tried to understand my behavior instead of getting angry with myself. This analysis helped me set up a better reward system and become conscious of behavioral patterns I wanted to change. The next time you do a self-analysis on the spot, find out why you fall into certain patterns of behavior.

It's the only way to change. When you honestly address what to change, you have the opportunity to meet your issues head-on. And this is when you will kick ass in your life. In the next chapters you will read how I changed. I share my personal stories and then give you suggestions on how you can improve your life. I share how I got rid of my bullshit and as a result live a happier life.

....
Be brutally honest with yourself! Your precious life depends on it.
....

A person who risks nothing is like a flower that never blossoms. Be bold, and you will prosper. Thrive and do not waste your precious life. Promise this to your dear future waiting to be unfolded!

CHAPTER 2:

RESISTANCE

RULE OF THUMB: THE MORE IMPORTANT A CALL OR ACTION IS TO OUR SOUL'S EVOLUTION, THE MORE RESISTANCE WE FEEL TOWARD PURSUING IT.
—Steven Pressfield

It was an interesting whirlwind of thoughts that tried to block me from editing my book on this given morning. The main character of this tornado was nothing less than good old resistance, but this time he did not succeed! Resistance, you son of a B★, I am recognizing you now! As soon as I felt resistance trying to do its damage, I came up with opposing thoughts. The ones that helped me beat this motherfucker.

Resistance shows up as fear, perfectionism, doubt, distraction, pain, procrastination, self-sabotage, denial, inaction, or simply not being honest with yourself. It appears in many forms, unfortunately, but when acknowledged for what it is, it can be conquered.

I started editing and felt anger forming inside of me. I felt a slight irritation toward my editor. She had given me comments on my second draft. Why did she write as a comment that she needed to know "more of me" in the book? Had I not said enough private things already? I thought I had. Did I have to go totally naked? WTF! Resistance showed up as anger. Often when angry we stop doing what we should be doing. I then thought. No! No! No! She is right, and your resistance is trying to block you from showing the deeper experiences from your life and creating more openness as a result in your book.

Then I felt tired. I felt impatience forming in my body. Why was my book not done yet? I do not like the editing process—I like the creating part more! The book felt like a mountain that was too high to climb. Now resistance showed up as impatience. When feeling impatient you just want to drop it all and do something else, like eat ice cream, for instance, because what is the use? Then I thought, "Wrong again! Start small and do not think about wanting to edit a book of more than two hundred pages at once. Focus on correcting one page at a time! Just one page, and then move forward with patience."

Then I looked at the layers of my stomach. I thought about the book *The Power of Habit* I had read. I learned from it, so shouldn't I, at this point, have a flat stomach? When would I finally do it all, instead of falling back into old and destructive behavior? Resistance showed up as distraction, and it was self-sabotaging. Then I told myself that things take time. My three-layered stomach, which took thirty years to form, would not disappear in five days. In this instance it was my belly, but with everything hard to change, time and patience are our saviors. Then I looked up inspiring videos about mind power. I learned how our subconscious mind has a powerful engine that moves it forward. Our willpower, on the other hand, is the one making lasting changes, but it is paddling in a tiny boat without a powerful engine. We need to influence our willpower, but the engine, with our emotions, is often stronger than our willpower. Rationality often loses, so we have to build a stronger *why*—the reason we do what we do.

By increasing your *why* level, you will make it so your emotions do not always take over your rationality. "Slow and effective, Tania!" I told myself to be okay with the process, to love pain instead of resisting it. Pain is my personal god. Pain is my healer. Pain will rescue me and help me become the woman of my dreams.

Resistance is a deadly force. Marriages collapse, dreams shatter, visions are torn apart, sadness is sprung, and lots of tears shed because resistance conquered us, instead of us conquering resistance. I believe we all can conquer resistance; it's one of the most important things to reckon with.

Resistance Is Your Enemy

Why is resistance used as an excuse? Why don't we do things that would help us, and instead do ridiculous things that keep us from truly living? Why do we flee from our freedom and instead lock ourselves up?

The sad truth is, we are afraid of our light. We are afraid to succeed. We are afraid of our beauty. We are afraid to get rid of our bullshit because it is what we know. We are afraid to kick ass and live the best life ever. What if we became what our hearts wanted? What if we became elevated? What if we became that badass, a person who found their destiny and their truth, a person who found the power deep inside they knew they had? What if we stopped listening to the naysayers around us and ventured out on our own? What if we stopped delaying and made our precious life breaths worthy? What if we gave the world all we have?

> We are afraid of our light and do the unimaginable to destroy it.

We are afraid of succeeding, and therefore hide in our caves, postpone more, and tell ourselves that it was just not in the stars. Be a warrior with your own created light and slay the dragon of destruction. You have to acknowledge resistance for what it is, but then fight it.

Fight it by telling yourself that *yes* you can succeed. *Yes*, you are worthy of love. *Yes*, you can be a force that creates beauty in this world. *Yes*, you will make a difference. Fight it hard with boldness and strength. Fight it smart. Resistance is like the devil on our shoulders trying to guide us to places he wants to visit, places where he feels comfortable. Unfortunately, those are not the places where our dreams grow. Those are places that bring us more delay, delay we get forced into by this evil entity. It rains outside, so be it. Rain is fucking great. You can still go for a run. Resistance will tell you to cozy up in bed instead of putting your scheduled run in. Your check has not arrived yet? Do you panic, get restless, and overeat? Resistance wants you to. It tells you that you are inadequate and never will have enough financial resources. Resistance plays a dirty fucking game and often wins because we get weak and give up.

Instead, what could you learn while waiting for your pay to come? What does it matter that a guy has not called you back? Maybe he is busy, and if he does not call you back at all, leave him. Resistance will tell you that you are not worthy of a relationship. Move on; there are millions of potential lovers in this world. I am sure you'll find kinder versions out there. You can always go and find many of them in Italy. Do not let resistance seduce you with its tempting voice. It is a fucking destroyer.

Stop Creating a Huge Pile of Excuses

Excuses can build up into a gigantic pile, a pile that becomes so problematic that it becomes your reality instead of the reality you want. This huge pile comes crashing down, keeping you from truly living, and you know it needs to stop. However, until you conquer resistance, you create more piles of excuses. Replacing your excuses with your dreams can stop this sabotaging routine.

Build Dreams Instead

If you can conquer resistance by finishing what is important to you, you will be able to beat it. Just that first one! That first book, that first song, that first project. Be the David who beat Goliath, and soar to greater heights. Do something you thought was impossible. We only have one life, and resistance is our enemy.

....

Resistance is invisible.
Resistance is a trickster.
Resistance is a parasite.
Resistance makes you weak.
....

Steven Pressfield's books *The War of Art* and *Do the Work* are the best books about resistance. When I need a jolt of energy and a kick in my butt, I read his books. They should be mandatory reading for anybody that experiences resistance.

He wrote in *The War of Art* that "Most of us have two lives. The life we live, and the unlived life within us. Between the two stands resistance."

These two books showed me how big resistance was. It was a power so destructive, so invisible, so ever changing, and so present in almost all the fabric of our lives. His books gave me clarity and defined resistance. Resistance is bigger than the biggest planet out there.

It wants to kill our dreams and bury us alive.

But at the same time, the two books full of wisdom and practicality told me who generated this evil force. "Resistance arises from within," Steven said. It was *me*. I was the one creating it, keeping it alive, and feeding it the best nutrition in the world so it stayed alive. Therefore, only I, David, could kill this Goliath called resistance. The solution Steven gave was, in hindsight, easier for me to do than I thought. I had to turn into a pro. I had to start writing, show up, and do the fucking work.

> Resistance hates it when we turn pro and do the fucking work.

While reading his books, I saw visuals appear in my imagination that showed me doing my job as a writer. I saw a vision of what I looked like being a pro. There comes a time when you have to kill this evil entity called resistance and say goodbye to the world of amateurism that has kept you from living your dreams and become a pro. I am forever grateful for Steven for diving so deeply into this subject matter that it now helps many of us who are looking for an effective tool to beat resistance's power once and for all.

Resistance's Ugly Head in My "Past" Life
I felt lots of resistance in my life, especially when I was in my twenties and thirties. I was in a rut instead

of waking up and telling myself that I was living a bullshit life. I did not face my fears, see the truth, and figure things out. I was not honest with myself.

Instead I gave in to more delay. I lived up to other people's idea of who I was supposed to be. They loved me as a bank manager, selling many of their products and making the bank lots of money. Instead I had dreams of being an artist. Art is where I belonged, not in a bank office where the walls were closing in on me. Luckily, I conquered my resistance and left, and it still feels damn good.

I want you to have a life with no resistance, or as little as possible. We often do not know it is resistance when it shows up. We think it is "okay" to continue how we are, or think it is normal not to change. For instance, when we have a prestigious job with lots of financial growth attached, resistance tells us, "You are crazy to let go of this high-paying job to become a writer, an actress, an illustrator, a painter, a chef, a teacher, a foreign tour guide, a photographer, a traveler, or an explorer."

You Have to Kill Resistance

Fucking kill this bastard! Look it in the eyes and say, "No more! I want you out!" The biggest waste to humanity is when we do not do what we are supposed to be doing. Pain will stack up for years, and when you are older, you will feel regret. This regret is like a tsunami. You do not see it coming, but when it comes, it crushes everything and causes pain and grief. Do not let the tsunami of regret crush you into a million pieces. You have to be aware when resistance pops up its ugly head and wants to swallow you in its abyss and kidnap your dreams.

I remember one morning in LA, after four days of constant rain, I was fed up with being inside and thought, "I am going out." I wore my sexy black boots I never get to wear, because it is almost always hot in LA, and walked a half-mile to a coffee shop to have my favorite drink, only to find out that it was closed because of the rain. I went to another coffee shop and started writing this chapter about resistance.

Resistance has kidnapped precious time in my life. From a young age I wanted to become an actress. Living in the Netherlands, I was intrigued by the American TV series *Dynasty* and *Dallas*. I even named my dog after Bobby Ewing, a character on the show; I had a major crush on him. My dog Bobby and I often watched American TV series, and I dreamed about one day walking on the beautiful stairs they showed in the show. I made my first attempt at acting and modeling when I was sixteen, shortly after leaving my parents' house. I became the model of the week and was on TV for a week. Instead of letting it skyrocketing me, I let it stop me.

Family and Friends Can Sabotage

My family was ashamed of me doing this. In their culture it was inappropriate to be shown in sexy clothes with strangers watching. I did not pursue acting hard enough after this first job, because the resistance in me did not want to hurt my family. I pleased them instead of going after my dreams. I gave up for years. I moved to Amsterdam and started working at the bank. But it wasn't long before destiny came knocking at my door again.

At the bank I worked at, there was a client who had a big production company, Shooting Star Film Company. Dave, the founder, is a super-nice guy who was at the beginning of his career. One day he came into the bank, smiled, and said his usual hello. He said they were shooting a music video and asked if I wanted to come and see it. I thought this was my moment to be brave, and I said I would only visit if I could be in the video. He said, "Sure, we will make a role for you."

I became the love interest of the main character in a music video. The group was called Diamond, and the main singer put a scarf around my neck and pulled me toward him and then tried to kiss me. I swooned and felt great. Excitement burst in my body and warmed me up on that cold bridge where we shot the video. I had not only made a valuable connection in the film business, but I also had a credit as an actress on my acting resume now: Tania, the love interest of R&B group Diamond in the United States! I felt great. I had beat resistance and was fearless when I asked to be in the video.

Then resistance sneaked into my life again. The bank loved my work ethic and asked me to go to business school. They would pay for everything. I would continue to work and attend classes in the evenings. I went to school in the evenings for five years, three to four evenings a week, while also having a full-time job. This was hard because I had no time left to socialize or do anything acting related. Resistance won again. I let the bank dictate how my life went instead of pursuing my acting career after filming that video.

I finished business school and got promoted to team leader. They created this position especially for me because they saw my potential. I was now a manager, and because they loved me, they suggested I should go to another business school and they would also pay for this one. Again, I went with it and did it for another three years.

I was twenty-five when I started the second business school, and was not happy at all, but thought, "Let me just finish this and get it over with." I kept going till I hit a breaking point. I hit a major wall because I was not living the life I wanted. I burned out. A full-time job as a manager, business school, and acting classes on the weekends were too much for me.

I missed acting, so I had begun classes again on the weekends. Then one day I was sitting at home and the horrible news came in that Princess Diana was killed. I remember thinking that life was too short. I needed to do what I loved and not what others thought I should do. Shortly after, I decided to quit the bank, stop attending the second business school, and move to America to become an actress. I would attend acting school there, instead of wasting more time. It had taken me ten years from that R&B video with Diamond to move to the city where acting dreams are made. I wasted years because resistance always took over. It had this invisible power, and I had not realized yet how strong it was.

I want you to take this force seriously, this fucked-up force; you will waste many years, and it is the ultimate death trap.

> Remember that by not taking risks, you end up risking it all.

A life without risks is a worthless life. You will be like other timid souls who have talked about big dreams, fantasies, visions, and inspirations, but have not done enough to bring them alive. Do not be tempted by shining temporary diamonds sparkling in front of you and telling you to stay. Quit a job you hate and do what makes your heart sing. Here are more suggestions on how to beat resistance.

Tell Yourself, "So What?" When Feeling Resistance

When resistance rears up with its ugly head and makes you stagnate, say, "So what that this or that is happening?" Many people are less fortunate and still go into the arena to fight. Work with what you have. You have to do something. Do not sit at home and let precious time go to waste. Tell yourself a mantra. Say it out loud. Sing it. Write it down and let "So what?" motivate and guide you to make a start and not kill your dreams.

Watch Inspirational Videos of Others

Many people have had harder times, but they are thriving. I am thinking of the poem from Maya Angelou, "Still I Rise." Read it. It will help and give you jolts of power. One morning I watched the TED Talk of Doctor B.J. Miller, who lost three limbs but is still out there fighting for a higher cause. He talked about how a nurse brought a snowball into the hospital and gave it to him. He almost choked when talking about it. He was in a burn unit for months and could not go outside to pick up something as simple as snow. In the TED Talk he said, "And one night, it began to snow outside. I remember my nurses complaining about driving through it. And there was no window in my room, but it was great just to imagine it coming down all sticky. The next day, one of my nurses smuggled in a snowball for me. She brought it into the unit. I cannot tell you the rapture I felt holding that in my hand and the coldness dripping onto my burning skin; the miracle of it all, the fascination as I watched it melt and turn into water. In that moment, just being any part of this planet in this universe mattered more to me than whether I lived or died. That little snowball packed all the inspiration I needed to both try to live and be okay if I did not."

Snow became a cherished thing. This snowball had

a deeper meaning for him. We often forget to appreciate the small things. We are lucky to be able to walk around and play in the snow and hold it and feel the cold and throw it. We take many things for granted. When I feel sorry for myself, I go to Skid Row, a place in LA where a lot of the homeless live, and drive around. Seeing people fighting to stay alive, in the rain, shivering in the cold, and living in tents grounds me. I sometimes bake cookies for them and hand them out.

Gratitude Grounds

Remember to be grateful for having a healthy life and a roof over your head.

Millions on our planet are not that fortunate. We have so much but forget this often. Remind yourself of what all you have and be grateful for everything.

Feel Happiness Electrify

Another way to beat resistance is to feel jolts of happiness flow inside you. Do this by doing simple things that make you happy. Let your joy inspire you to feel good and keep resistance outside. Give yourself tiny rewards to boost your mood to get started. For me it is getting a smoothie or a Boba drink, or eating fruit. I love fruit. It makes me happy.

In *Twin Peaks*, Agent Cooper says to Harry Truman, "You know what you need to do every day? Give yourself a present." Reward yourself with small things to escape a nonaction mode and create. Find something that works for you.

Connect Strongly with Your Purpose

Why is what you want to do so important to you? For me, I could not waste more time and needed to bring my story to others who were also struggling. I wanted to lead by example. I could show others how I changed and got rid of my bullshit life, so they could do the same. I wished somebody had kicked me in the butt earlier in life, so I could have conquered resistance and finished my goals earlier. Feel the reason why you are doing it strongly in your body. Fill up with this important energy and let it feed your heart. Most importantly: start today.

Start *now*!

How Will You Be after Creating Your Masterpiece?

Feel how you positively influence people when you conquer resistance. You can be a role model for others. You can inspire them to go for it as well. I always say that individuals who have conquered their resistance created humanity's present beauty. Do it for your fellow humans and do it for yourself. Get to work today, please!

Not tomorrow and not the day after tomorrow.

"Now" Is the Word You Should Be Guided By

Resistance fucking wasted so many years of my life. I was unaware of its power till recently. I kicked that piece of shit out. Make a start today and get rid of this ugly beast.

CHAPTER 3:

MARATHONS AND VOLCANOES

TO ENJOY THE GLOW OF GOOD HEALTH, YOU MUST EXERCISE.
—Gene Tunney

I had had enough. In the mirror I saw a hanging stomach—actually, let me take that back; I saw three hanging stomachs on top of each other, three layered rolls stacked like the floors of a building. My upper legs were full of cellulite and looked like cottage cheese, and my upper arms were like soft taffy. My previous hourglass figure was one unattractive rectangle. Change was needed. I took pictures of my body, cried while looking at the green walls in my studio, and started exercising.

This might sound like not that big of a deal, but it was for me. I never loved exercising. In fact, I passionately hated it. In gym class, the kids would line up in a row, from tall to short. I was always at the end of the line, being the shortest, and never chosen first. At the end, when everybody else was chosen, the picker would say to the other team, "You can have her! Please take her for free." Well, they did not say the free part, but it felt that way for me. Especially with sports like basketball, tall people were desired. I hated the gym and wanted to get rid of my embarrassment in class.

I went as far as writing notes to the gym teacher and falsifying my dad's signature on them so I did not have to attend classes. I was innovative with the excuses and copied my dad's signature from my report card. They believed me. Looking back, I was already an actress but did not get paid for it yet. In fact, maybe I was a little criminal!

At twenty-five, still hating sports and feeling weak physically, I came up with a brilliant idea. I would sign up for a senior gym class, thinking that I could easily handle exercise with a class full of seniors. It was the magic pill for me. After one or two sessions at a regular gym, I always gave up. I thought I could keep up with the seniors, but I couldn't. They jumped around like butterflies overdosing on steroids. I left class with a hanging head. Exercising was not for me. My body could not handle physicality, and besides, I always pushed my heart rate to a dangerous zone by breathing too fast.

Decades went by with no exercising, but that August with my three-layered stomach, I decided to start running. I had a cute light green Adidas top and black shorts, and I had just started. It went well till I had the flu and gave up for months. I only ran when I felt inspired, but that is not how new habits stick. You have to implement a system and follow it.

A year later, I went through the same routine. I took pictures of my body, was unhappy, and started running. This time I ran more than the previous year. Everything went well till I felt pain in my right big toe. I went to a toe doctor to check it out. After paying him $160 for a ten-minute consultation, he said that I had nothing. He said it would go away by itself, like many things in life, with time and rest. "Really?" I thought, frustrated. "I have nothing? What do you mean I have nothing? I can feel this fucking pain. I am not making this up just to pay you $160 that I could not afford in the first place." I gave up on running again. I was not made for it. I had toe problems! I again had received proof that I could not do it. It turned out later that I was running with a size seven, my shoe size, but when running you must run with a size bigger than your actual size. Duh! I did not know this because I was still a miserable amateur.

Set a Daring Goal

I was downhearted, but I still wanted to change. I needed to do something drastic, something daring that would elevate me to another level. Something I could never do in a hundred years or have the capacity to do. Something that would skyrocket me to a level of physicality as if I had trained like a maniac for the last thirty years—an accelerated springboard that gave physical superpowers.

Find Your Volcano—An Active One if Up for a Challenge!

My answer came with lots of enthusiasm: I needed to hike a volcano. And not just a volcano, it had to be an active one, with spewing lava to run quickly away from, to make it more challenging and my exercise worthwhile. A girl has got to give herself big goals, right? An active volcano, it was! A girl I knew had just hiked the Stromboli volcano in Sicily, Italy, and had inspired me. I knew nothing about volcanoes and was not a hiker at all. I would hike maybe once in five years with a friend, but would be out of breath after three minutes and could not wait to stop. Seeing pictures of her hiking this volcano and holding lava stones in her hand did something to me internally. It activated a desire I had never experienced before. I knew that that was what I had to do.

She had hiked this volcano in July. I wrote in my notes on July 9, "Tania, hike Stromboli volcano." I gave myself a non-negotiable command. I learned that this is useful. Write down a command you have to follow. Write it in the third person, follow it, and throw all your excuses in the trash bin.

A month later I was in Sicily ready to hike an active volcano in the Aeolian Islands. The day we hiked was superhot. We left at six in the evening. I immediately started sweating, and I never sweat. We hiked with twenty people, and the first few minutes I was okay, but then we climbed up a very steep hill. I was cursing myself and thought, "What the hell am I doing here?" And why was the guide going so fast?

Did he think we were marathon sprinters? I had little hiking experience and felt weak and hot.

What kept me going was that if I could not finish this, I could not finish anything in my life. This was it. I had to persist for once with my exercising goals. I wanted to get rid of my three-layered belly that kept me away from dating and many other good things in life. I had booked flights, taken time off, and arranged an expensive last-minute accommodation, and I would be damned if I would not finish. When we got to 250 meters, the guide told us that anyone who wanted to go back had to go now. His coworker would bring them all back to town. Some people decided it was too hard and took him up on the offer. I did not want to go back. I would push through the pain once and for all. I would conquer this motherfucking Italian volcano. We kept going, and I was constantly in the last group.

When we got to 500 meters and it became steeper and steeper, I felt moments of wanting to give up. Luckily, we were with a group; if I was alone, I might have gone back. The heat, the steepness, the sweat I felt, my shallow breathing, and my swollen feet were not making it easier. I often thought about stopping this madness and going back and drinking Italian prosecco with a cute Italian instead.

One of the things that kept me going was the promise of active lava. Spewing lava was appealing to me. I always look for adventure and want to experience thrilling things. The other thing was just the sheer pride of having accomplished the feat. It was a hard trek, but it would be tougher to go back to LA and tell my friends that I gave up. "Keep going, TD; keep going," I told myself over and over as I progressed up the Stromboli volcano.

We eventually arrived at the top. It took more than three hours, and I am sure I slowed down the group. It was almost ten at night when we reached the top, and we stayed for only twenty minutes. The sky was cloudy, and we did not see much lava, which was unfortunate, but I only needed to see a little.

Something happened inside of me on the top of that volcano. A spiritual power flowed in my body, a strength that felt like unbendable steel. I had done something I believed impossible. I was excited, took pictures with the other hikers, and anticipated going back and having my glass of delicious Italian wine.

The hike back would be easy, I thought, because I could just slide down—a piece of cake, or in this case, a piece of a volcano. I was dead wrong. We had been hiking already for more than four hours. My feet started shaking; I had no control over them. My legs could not walk straight lines anymore, because of exhaustion. It got very dark, and my feet slipped and disappeared beneath the high piles of lava sand we had to walk through. I had to forcefully pull them out, which caused my shoes to fill up with the sand. I had to be hyperaware of where I stepped. The paths were tiny; one little misstep and you would fall into the abyss. Big stones were hidden in the lava sand, not visible because of the darkness. The hikers in the front would sometimes yell to warn us when a stone appeared, but that was not always possible. Sometimes they were far ahead. I was sweating and hot, and my legs had swollen. My hiking boots felt super tight, but I could not take them off. The pain would get worse, and I would be left behind. People wanted to go back since it was getting closer to midnight. We did not take breaks going down like we did when climbing up.

Finally, after midnight, we arrived back in town, and I was relieved. My body was sticky with sweat; my shoes were full of lava sand, and my legs shook uncontrollably like a marionette going crazy. My initial plan was to have a glass of Italian champagne after the hike, but it was not possible anymore. Everything was closed on Stromboli Island! "Oh well," I thought, "I'll walk back to my room, rest, and have champagne tomorrow." I had no food in the apartment because I had planned to get a meal at one of the restaurants. I only had a little bag of *tarallis*, small, round Italian crackers flavored with rosemary, that I bought earlier. I ate those crackers like they were fresh grilled shrimps with roasted potatoes and an Italian dessert to die for. Those crackers were the best I ever had in my life.

The next day I left early and was fulfilled. I had done it. I hiked an active volcano and was proud of myself. I felt like a superwoman. I did something that was impossible in my wildest dreams. "If I can hike for six hours," I thought, "What else can I do that I always thought was impossible?" I gazed at the volcano in the early morning and took the boat to the mainland of Italy. Nobody could take this experience away from me. It was now engraved in the cells of my body, and I would carry it with me my whole life. Within a month of writing my goal, I hiked it and conquered myself. Conquer yourself and then act fast. This is how I began to get my life back.

Always Pursue Difficult Things

I realized that to have an extraordinary life, something all of us can have, we have to pursue difficult things. When you do hard things, you earn self-respect. Accomplishing hard things propels us to higher levels. Ordinary people can take up impossible tasks they thought they could not handle.

One of the keys is forgetting everything you believed before. Common knowledge would say that a woman in her midforties, who never exercised, could not hike an active volcano in Italy. But I am telling you, it does not matter what has happened in your past. Work on a better now so it can become your grand future. Fill in your present with quality actions. A determined mind can take you far in life.

> Ordinary people can live extraordinary lives if they commit to doing hard things; set up goals, and then experience an explosive empowerment.

Rethink What You Think and What You Thought

What is hard is often smart. What is hard will change you for the better. If you can challenge yourself to do something hard, you will gain superpowers in the process. You will rewire your brain and change from a nonbeliever to a believer. I decided to hike more volcanoes, and I did—seven up to now. Not all were active ones, but I have many years to climb many more.

I decided to start running to get my exercise in. Running was something I could just do in my neighborhood. If you want to increase it a notch, you can do an epochal thing like a marathon—which I've also done.

First Marathon

Let me take you on the journey of my first marathon, while not being a runner. I went on a trip for nine days with J. He works in the Netherlands, and I was assigned to show him parts of the USA, as I was working as a tour director. J is a sweet, clever, and focused guy, and during our time together, we spoke about a variety of subjects. I was impressed by his vision and the way he stood in life. His main passion, besides traveling, was running marathons. He ran at least six per year, full and half ones.

"Six!" I screamed inside. "He must be a god or something. Who on earth can run so many?" What stuck with me were three things he said about running marathons during our trip. First, he said the strength you need during a marathon is mostly mental. Hearing this got me excited; physically, I was weak as pudding, but mentally I was strong. I could hardly run a minute, but I had mental resilience.

Second, he said that everything you wanted to know about yourself and did not know, you would find out during a marathon. Again, I was intrigued. I love to know things. I read a lot and enjoy contemplating what I've read; it is one of my main hobbies. I reflect about life, I think about my friends, I ponder about my family, I contemplate about the state of humanity, and I think about how to be a bigger giver. I am curious, and knowing things is a big part of my life, but I did not know myself completely. I did not know my limits and how far I could push myself. I sometimes do things that surprise me and then get disappointed with the outcome. What is more important than to know thyself?

Because of our conversation, I was already half in an imaginary future marathon. What would my psyche show me? What would I learn that would help me excel? We do not often get valuable information about ourselves in day-to-day life, because we do not stretch ourselves enough.

Then J mentioned the third reason why running a marathon is great. When you get to the twenty-second mile, you feel like a superhuman. You feel like you can fly and gain superpowers. I wanted to become superhuman. I *had* to do a marathon. There was no other way. The trip with J ended on June 1, and my birthday was on June 8. What usually happens around my birthday is that I reflect deeply the days before. This happened again on June 6 while sitting at one of my favorite coffee shops, Maru in Los Feliz. I drank my regular matcha latte; they serve the best in Los Angeles. I was calm, happy, and peaceful. I felt that I could conquer the world. I could do anything if I went for it full force.

Make It Specific with a Date

It was at that moment, sitting at the coffee shop at eleven thirty in the morning, when I wrote in my notes, "Tania, run a marathon." Again, I gave myself a command like I did with the volcano. First I wrote it with no date, but to succeed you have to make it specific. A deadline helps make it happen. I rewrote it, "Tania, run your first marathon in 2018!" At 11:35 a.m., I wrote my intention down, and at 2:30 p.m. I registered for my first marathon! I had no idea how to train or how long it would take to build the physical power for it, so I went on Google. It would take twenty-four weeks. Great, I thought! Then I searched, "What marathon is there in twenty-four weeks?" And then the Marathon of the Marathons showed up on my screen.

The first marathon started 2,500 years ago when the messenger Pheidippides ran to Athens to announce victory against the Persians. He died, unfortunately, upon arrival, but in his honor millions run them today. The Athens marathon starts in the town of Marathon, 26.2 miles away, and finishes in

Athens, Greece, in the marble Panathenaic Stadium, 2,500 years old and also the birthplace of the Olympics. I was in awe. I did not expect this to come up.

I imagined running a marathon close to home to make it easier for myself, where I knew the streets and did not have to travel across the world. But there was no way back. I was determined and wanted to have that superhuman feeling and fly like a goddess in the olive fields of Greece.

I immediately went to the Greek website of this Authentic Marathon and signed up. It was easy to do, and I only paid a hundred bucks! I signed up at 2:30 p.m., barely three hours between ideation and registration.

Do Not Overthink, and Act Fast

Things can be done fast in life, if you don't overthink and just go for it. I was in an elevated state and had to strike while the iron was hot. The next day, I thought, "Let me research this marathon." It said on Wikipedia that it was one of the hardest in the world. It was a marathon with a lot of hills; it was the marathon with the lowest percentage of women signing up. "Oh my freaking God," I thought. "What have I done? I am out of my mind to do this." I was glad I did not know this the previous day. I would have chosen an easier one. Being naive is sometimes your best friend in situations like this. I told myself, "I am going to make this happen." One of my favorite words is *ginesthoi*. It is a Greek word written by

Cleopatra on the only sheet of paper we have left from her in her handwriting, and it means "make it happen."

I was going to make it happen. I was going to run the Authentic Marathon and feel the wind of ancient history around me. And I was going to go where Cleopatra received her superpowers and lived. I needed a plan because as a non-runner, I wanted to take this seriously and make sure I finished. A trainer made me a schedule; I bought new running shoes and started running. I ran every other day till I was able to run six miles, and then I got injured. I was out for weeks. I followed the schedule, but in hindsight it was too ambitious. I was a beginner, and the plan was more tailored to an experienced runner. I ran fewer miles to stay injury-free.

Slow Down

My golden tip for you is not to go too fast in the beginning of your training for a marathon. (Or any new venture—whether it's exercise or travel or learning something new—give yourself time!) Going slow is wise. You do not have to run a marathon or hike an active volcano to become physically fit and strong, but you have to do something outside your comfort zone, so you can live a kick-ass life. This newly gained energy will spill over positively into other areas of your life. Find something fun to do. Or do a combination of challenging and fun. I combined the hard part of exercising with the fun part of traveling abroad for it. That was the golden answer for me. I now feel better after every workout.

City of Marathon to City of Athens

Running the Athens Marathon is one of my most cherished experiences. The hills, the warmth of the Greek people, and the excellent organization made it in the top five most important happenings in my life. There were hundreds of energetic, focused, passionate runners who made me feel calm. I did not have to be afraid—I *would* finish. The wonderful thing about the Athens Marathon is that the organization gives everybody eight hours to run it. You can walk it if that is all you can do. The beginning is flat, but then the famous hills appear, which make it challenging, but the smiling families on the side of the roads, giving you high fives and offering needed encouragement, keep you going. It was hotter than expected, which was not easy. But again, like with my first volcano, I was not going to be defeated. I would conquer the Athens Marathon even if I had to crawl over the finish line. Luckily I did not have to do that. The run was not easy. Wikipedia made me slightly frightened, but in hindsight it was not needed.

The last part of the marathon is easier, as it's all downhill. The feeling at the finish line is impossible to describe. Your pain is infused with happiness and power. You experience pure joy. Then the precious medal is the cherry on the top. The beautifully designed Athens medal feels like pure magic in your hands. You feel like you have received a golden bar you get to keep. You enriched yourself. You felt ancient history take part of you, and then you tell yourself that this will not be the last one you will run. In your heart you have already signed up for the next one next year. Trust me, it will not be your last Athens Marathon. To all the Greek people and the organization, thank you for your passion for your marathon and the divine support you gave to us runners.

You Can Do It—I Believe in You

A healthy mind cannot function without a healthy body. It took me forty years to love exercise. Do not negotiate whether you should do something in the morning or not. Do not start a dialogue with your resistance; instead, just start doing some sort of exercise. If you are doing some activity already, kudos to you. If not, then I hope that I've convinced you that even somebody like me, who couldn't handle senior gym class, is now able to enjoy physical activities.

CHAPTER 4:

EATING HABITS

> THE MORE YOU EAT, THE LESS FLAVOR;
> THE LESS YOU EAT, THE MORE FLAVOR.
> —Chinese Proverb

I have not conquered this superpower yet, but this is what I have learned so far:

To live an optimal life, your relationship with food must be good. This doesn't mean you have to be super thin or go on a diet. It means respecting your health in relation to eating.

I struggled to have a healthy relationship with food for a long time. My derailed relationship started when I was a young kid. I loved food, but I often overate.

Food was my buddy that was always present when I needed it most.

Feeling sad? There were two pints of ice cream. Feeling lonely? There was a whole cherry pie. Felt stuck in life? Voila, a bag with buttery caramels gave me a high.

My relationship with food was complex. I am a foodie, so it's a double challenge. Besides using food as a medicine to heal, I also experience the beauty of food, being an epicurean at heart. I love the thousands of different taste profiles. I love the diversity and the excitement that food brings to the table. I love how alive it makes me feel. Salty, sugary, tart, sour, or mixed, all flavors make my heart beat faster and happier. But anything with the words *too much* in front of it is not good.

Young Food Habits Stick

When I was a child, I remember my mom hiding food from me in the basement. I was in a constant state of hunger and would eat everything, so she locked it up with a key she hid in a secret place. As soon as she left the house I would search in every minuscule spot to find that key. Sometimes it took hours, and sometimes it took minutes, but I usually found the treasured key. The challenge was to eat without leaving any traces. For example, if there were pies in the basement, I would cut a tiny slice from each piece, about a half-inch, and then push the parts back together to form a circle again, like nothing was taken out.

There was also a big can of olives. I am talking gigantic olives here, big juicy green Spanish olives; you commit a felony for eating them. When something was tasty, I never seemed to have enough. One day I went into the basement again, and when I grabbed the inside of the can, greedily pulling out a delicious olive, I cut my finger at the top and was bleeding. I put saliva on my finger, pinched it to stop the bleeding, and closed the can. I did not realize, in my haste, that blood had dripped on the side of the can. I rushed upstairs because my mom could come back at any minute. Sometimes she only went to the local grocery store and was back in merely twenty minutes.

Later, after she had returned, she summoned me and said that I had gone into the basement. I denied it, of course, being a little nine-year-old, but she said firmly that I had. I denied again. She then took me to the basement and showed me the blood that was now hardened on the side of the can. Denying was impossible now. My damn blood had betrayed me. I had to be more careful next time.

The Bakery on the Corner Was Pie-licious

Another incident occurred at our local bakery. They often organized food competitions. The person who ate a full French baguette the fastest would win.

Guess who was the winner? The prize was a huge fresh-baked pie. I was extremely proud when I won; I pushed that whole French baguette into my mouth without chewing on it. I am amazed I did not choke. There weren't many qualities I had as a kid, but sticking a humongous baguette in my mouth and eating it like there was no tomorrow was one of my skills. My mom was angry when I brought the pie home. She said neighbors would think I was not getting fed enough. I was confused and hurt. I felt proud that I won, partly because I love winning, and partly because I wanted my mom to be proud that I won a delicious pie, but her disapproval stopped me from participating in more eating competitions.

Using Food as a Painkiller

My complex relationship with food started at a young age. I always thought there was not enough food around, and when you feel deprived, you want more. When I left my parents' house, I had a lot of pain inside of me. This pain was often unsustainable, and I experienced relief through overeating. Some overdrink, some do drugs, some go to parties, but my addiction was food. For more than thirty years it was my best friend, that initially helped me, but after I stuffed myself, would make me miserable. It was a double-edged sword that I could not live without. This relationship had to change. The cause was psychological: I had not forgiven individuals who hurt me, so therefore I often overate.

The moment I started forgiving myself and others was when my relationship with food improved. Now I try to eat when I am hungry. I hardly overeat anymore, and I cook a lot. My dishes come out like little paintings, so it's a creative outlet. I mix the ingredients like a painter and feel delighted when the outcome shows up on my plate. Food has transformed from being a "fill me up now" kind of thing, because of feeling emotional, to eating when I am hungry.

I am not healed yet. It is an ongoing process, but

a more manageable one. I still experience challenges, but I understand them better. Trigger points stay, so it is wise to make them sustainable. That is why having a good relationship with food will give you a superpower. What can you do to have a better relationship with food? Here is what I did and still do.

Write Your Family Food Habit Story

How did your family or the people you grew up with act toward food? Did they think it was abundant, or was it lacking? Did they let you eat everything you wanted, or were you controlled in your food intake? Did your mom diet? Did any of your siblings have food challenges, and were you influenced by them? Do you believe food is only nutrition, or medicine too? This exercise will give you important insights about your relationship with food. You might have unconsciously put away thoughts and labeled them as unimportant. But this is huge. The environment we were raised in and especially the ideas around food become imprints in our life.

Control Buying and Taking It Home

Most important, and this is easier said than done, is to not buy unhealthy items in the first place.

Let go of the urge to stock up. Hamsters are cute, but we do not have to copy their behavior of stockpiling food like there is no tomorrow. If you are driving around, for instance, and you tell yourself to go to the European delicatessen store twenty-five miles away to buy European candies, stop, rethink, and go get a healthy smoothie instead.

This happened to me a few days ago, so it is still fresh in my mind. Do not purchase chocolate, candy, or any other sugary overload and store them in your house in the first place. Buy them for special occasions or for rewards when you have done something you are proud of. Then treat yourself, enjoy it, and don't feel guilty about eating it.

What Are the Healthy Snacks Out There?

You can buy healthier snacks. For instance, fresh dates are amazing; they are made by nature, are naturally sweet, are good for you, and are filling. Buy eight ounces of dates and eat them as your snack for the rest of the week. Also, I love pomegranates. Pomegranates are magical things. Their name, the form, and the color make them unique. They take forever to peel, are delicious, and keep you occupied while peeling, so you let go of other unhealthy stuff.

Slow Down Food Intake

Eating more slowly is also important for developing a better relationship with food. Sit down when you eat. Observe your meal and surroundings, and enjoy your food. Chew slowly while feeling grateful that you have this abundance. If you can take the time to savor your meal, you will feel less hungry and develop a better connection with your food.

Clean to Stop Temptation

After dinner I use a water picker to clean my teeth. They are clean for the evening, and eating is over. You do not want to mess up sparkling clean teeth. Sometimes I drink tea or another healthy drink, but no regular foods after my cleaning. This habit changed my eating patterns and keeps me from overeating in the evening.

Want to Sleep Better and Live Longer?

For better sleep, I stopped eating after seven, three hours before going to bed. Healthy habits give you a longer life. Methuselah is a figure in Judaism, Christianity, and Islam who became super old. I wonder what he ate, by the way. Did he eat all his vegetables? Did he count his calories? He lived over 900 years, so he must have eaten well. I'm not sure if we all want to be Methuselah waking up on a particular day and thinking, "I just turned 969 years old today. Where are all my friends? I miss them!" but having a long and healthy life is desirable.

We can do this if we make the right food intake a priority and nurture our bodies. What sense does it make to grow older, but feel weak and have countless ailments because we did not give our bodies the right fuels?

Look at the Mediterranean Countries

In places like Italy and Greece, they eat great, have fewer heart attacks, and have a balanced food intake.

My grandparents were both Mediterranean farmers and lived to be more than a hundred years old. They worked hard and ate well. Let us be inspired by what people in the Mediterranean do and replicate that.

Japan Knows How to Do It Too!

Or let us look at our Japanese friends. People in Japan typically have long lives. In fact, they have the longest life expectancy in the world. They drink lots of green tea, eat seafood, and eat smaller portions. I am a big fan of matcha latte, so thank you, Japan, for making this for me to enjoy!

Take *Dieting* Out of Your Vocabulary

Dieting does not work. Initially you lose some weight, but it will often come back. Trust me, I have tried every diet out there. My relationship with food was complex, but when I stopped dieting I finally felt more in control. I threw my scale away and felt liberated. Throw that happiness-sucker out of your house!

In the end, it simply comes down to eating better foods, in smaller portions, in a slower way, and eating more colorful fruits and vegetables. I love making my own healthy smoothies at home. For optimum health, go to bed earlier and eat less. That is the magic trick. You do not have to count calories obsessively; it will only make you depressed.

Here is to happier eating!

CHAPTER 5:

BETTER YOUR THINKING

WE ARE SHAPED BY OUR THOUGHTS; WE BECOME WHAT WE THINK.
—Buddha

Better thinking makes us resilient. A rich philosophy leads to a miraculous life and provides an existence full of bliss, self-respect, and worthy accomplishments. When we improve our thinking, we become happier. Your thoughts determine who you are, and this means that your thoughts shape your life. We invent ourselves through our thinking.

> It's an amazing concept. You determine who you are by what you think.

What if we looked deep in our hearts, focused on loving ourselves, and guided our thoughts toward becoming better people? What if we took our marvelous lives a notch higher and committed to improving ourselves? What if we became aware that our time is not limitless and cherished the limited time left? Our thinking is the concrete building block that forms the basis of our human experience.

> Just like Atlas is holding the earth up high, we can hold our thinking at a higher level.

Did you know that thinking causes 90 percent of our problems? When I read this shocking statistic, I was blown away. It is therefore super important to think well. Make sure to empower yourself instead of thinking yourself into the gutter.

How to think better so you can kick ass in your life:

1. **It starts with your words.** Instead of using language related to failure, realize you are a contender, you are trying! You are an art project in the making. You are creating yourself, so please be patient. Use words that evoke strength, help you progress, are success-oriented, and bring power.
2. **Believe that your thinking is special because you are unique**. There is only one of you here on earth, and most of our thoughts are divine. Cherish that and make it a habit to hold thoughts that help you grow and stay calm. Focusing on a calm

state of mind will help ward off stress, which can elevate your thinking.
3. **Keep negative thoughts away.** We cannot always push our negative thoughts to the side, but do not empower them either! Let them gently flow away. Acknowledge them, but do not strengthen them by turning them into an ancient Roman fort.
4. **Confront your fears so you can open yourself up to daring possibilities.** Realize that life is not endless. Your time on earth is limited, so why not think the most amazing thoughts instead? You are a gift living on this earth. You are magical, and we need your unique thoughts.

....
Believe you deserve to think well and that you are smart.
....

Love Yourself More so You Will Think Better

I believe our best thinking happens when we commit to loving ourselves.

If you respect yourself more, your mind will blossom with nurturing thoughts. You will believe you are worthy of greatness and will not accept negative thoughts about yourself. Loving yourself brings confidence and joy. Let go of your crazy thinking! Let go of the negative thinking monster that wants to ruin your life!

> Think you are amazing, and your life will be incredible.

Then the contradictory part, because we humans are often more complex than we realize:

Do Not Believe Everything You Think

Our thoughts often make us feel worse about ourselves. Just one negative thought can kick off counterproductive thinking. We then look for evidence to support that first faulty thought, and before we know it, we have activated a huge avalanche of negativity that comes crashing down like a row of dominos. This domino effect keeps going strong till we replace it with positive thoughts that will help us. But why set up this domino effect in the first place? Why not correct ourselves before we make that first domino tile fall? Awareness is key; being in tune with your thinking is the first step toward living the life you want.

> Just because we think something does not mean it is true!

We as a species can fall into the trap of doomed thinking. And the amazing thing is that most of the horrible things we imagine never come true! Many dramas play out in our heads that never make their way into real life. They belong on stage, not in our mind. Do not fall into this nasty trap. Always keep your thinking in check. Ask yourself if it is true what you are thinking now. Or is it fear or maybe laziness speaking?

> The cause of our unhappiness is hopeless thinking.

We are related to the world by the way we think. Power is gained when we can take control of our thought process and flourish instead of degrading to lower levels of consciousness. Guide your mind into the most perfect stream in a river, a river that nourishes the fish, the plants, the beaver, the fisherman, the grass, the butterflies, and the mighty soil that keeps us all alive.

> What we focus thinking on, that we will become.

Focus on finding solutions in times of trouble instead of giving up. You can decide what your life is going to be. Your thoughts are powerful, and you can shape them to make your goals a reality. It takes discipline to guide your brain to fertile thoughts, and often you have to shift your perspective to get there.

> You are the master of this one pound of magic in your head.

Overthinking Is Like a Nasty Swamp

When you overthink, you get sucked into a horrid swamp that likes to keep you in the muck. Wallowing in the mire (that is, overthinking) keeps you from focusing on what you want. It keeps you from being productive. And it can keep you from your happiness.

Overloading or overwhelming yourself with many thoughts at the same time keeps you from truth and clarity. It's a distraction that holds you back from living your best life. And it can cause anxiety. However, this sort of thinking can often be addictive; it feels like thinking, but it doesn't get you anywhere. There are many reasons to overthink a situation, and often it's because we don't want to be in the present.

The first step to stopping this pattern is breaking down your thoughts. Instead of wallowing in them, ask yourself what they mean and what could happen. Take a rational approach, and use small steps to find the reality in the situation.

When you achieve clarity, your irrational thoughts sink to the bottom while the truth meets you at the surface. Sometimes it just takes awareness; though the swamp is thick and murky and seems like a trap you can't get out of, all you have to do is take a few steps, and you're out of the mud.

We often overthink about these things:

- Our self
- The future
- The past
- Our current reality

But happiness appears in abundant proportions when our thinking is aligned with truth and clarity instead of the murky swamp of overthinking.

How Do Great Minds Think Differently?

Effective, skilled thinkers know how to pick the juiciest fruits in life. They think long term, reach for their goals, and constantly re-evaluate themselves. They are the top athletes, the superstar actors, the leaders, the artists, and the misfits. They want to know how to improve themselves daily. Thinking effectively is the fastest path to living a gratifying, outstanding, and fulfilling life, and it will help you achieve multitudes.

The more awareness we have around our thoughts, the nobler life we create for the world. When you change your thinking and know what you deserve, your life will be remarkable and full of adventure. You do not have to be a genius to think differently. You just have to challenge the common wisdom out there and see correlations that others do not see.

I once met a famous soccer player, who I went on a few dates with. He asked what my goal in life was.

I realized I had none, zero goals, besides working. I was employed and thought that was what life was about: Get a job and keep it no matter what. Do not take risks. Commit to a long career in finance and then eventually buy a house, settle down, grow old, retire, and then die. My goals were all about making the bank people happy. His questioning of my goals and my absence of clarity made me rethink my life and connect the dots that were flying around like unguided projectiles. I had followed a path that others made for me—what if I created a new reality with my thinking?

> He made me think differently. Surround yourself with unique thinkers. They will help you realize your limitless possibilities.

First Thought

I think, I rethink, I overthink, and sometimes, I do not think at all, which is a blessing, too, but that is a topic for another time.

My first thought that I recall came when I was four in Maastricht, a city in the Netherlands. My mom and I had just moved to the Netherlands to join my dad. It was a chilly day in November in this newly adopted country. Everything was a culture shock for me, but I adjusted fast. I was looking through the cream-colored curtains hanging in the living room and desperately wanted to get out to explore the neighborhood. I felt adventure calling and pulling me with an invisible force away from the couch. My first thought came with a clear desire: "I want to get out and explore!"

Why was I locked up? I wanted freedom, before I knew what freedom even was. I told my mom I wanted to go out alone. She shook her head, and her face showed without words that my request was a no-no. She was worried I would get lost, or maybe kidnapped by strangers.

However, that thought was the start of something for me. My explorer's mindset was born through this thought. I set my mind on discovering the world, and nobody would stop me, not even a worrying mom. I wanted to get the hell out and see the world, starting at the age of four, and still do to this day. That feeling stayed with me for the rest of my life.

That is how powerful a first thought can be.

Our thoughts determine our life.

What Was Your First Thought?

Did your first thought decide your trajectory in life? Was it beneficial when you look back on it now? Try to bring that first thought back. Think deeply and visualize when it happened. You will receive valuable information.

I compare productive thinking skills to coming up with a signature dish. You cook with certain ingredients and get certain outcomes. The first time you make a recipe, it might not taste great, because you don't use quality ingredients or know exactly what you're doing yet. But the next time you make it, since you've made it before, you know what works, and it comes out very well. Then you can branch out and improvise, and it's still delicious. This is how effective thinking happens too. First you think primitively, unfamiliar with the thought recipe, and then when you know better, you do better. You make better choices and think better thoughts. You think with a wider overview.

Cook It Up with Imagination Stirred In!

Einstein is famous for saying, "Imagination is more important than knowledge." With imagination mixed in, your thoughts can flourish into vibrant ideas that lead to concrete actions. Dream big, be open, fantasize, think without limitations, and build those sandcastles to the highest levels possible! Do not listen to the naysayers or negative folks. Surround yourself with people who are big and imaginative thinkers who act on their beliefs. Their inspiration will help you live your life to the fullest, flourishing a million times over.

Many smart thinkers have touched on the importance of imagination, but how do you think brilliantly? Use lots of pictures. The human brain thinks in terms of visuals. It is not letters that float in your mind, but pictures. Visual thinking is effective.

I started a vision board recently. I look at it every day, and it empowers me when I see the events I aspire to accomplish. Come up with exciting visuals and let them marinate in your mind, things you want to materialize in your life. Find pictures and put them on a big sheet of paper. I have pictures of Picasso on my vision board and look at him every day. I ask, "What Picasso would do in my situation?" The answer: He would create like a motherfucker and stop worrying. Be your own Picasso or Leonardo da Vinci.

Do Your Own Thinking

An important starting point is to do the thinking yourself. We often copy thinking and behavior by observing others. It is fine to do that to a certain extent, and others can inspire us, **but never become lazy with something as important as your thinking**. I always had a strong drive, because I thought for myself first. I was not going to take anything for granted, without questioning it first. Is what this person told me true? Could it be wrong? Could it be a half-truth, and they do not know? Is the person telling me this because they have an agenda?

Celebrate Contrarian Thinking

My contrarian thinking caused friction with teachers and family, but it showed me valuable perspectives.

Imagine living in a small town, and having a desire to leave. Most likely when you talk with neighbors, friends, or family, and especially to the ones content living there, you get the advice to stay. The advice is filtered through their lenses that life is good there. Listening to them will not help you move. I lived in a smaller city, and when I wanted to venture out, people told me it would be dangerous and I would get killed in the big city! If I listened, I never would have moved.

I did my deep thinking and knew I needed to leave the nest to find my truth. Not every big city is dangerous, and if it was, I was not going to be in the bad neighborhoods. The exciting potential world I saw behind those cream-colored curtains could not be found in my current place. This is why it is so important to always develop your own thinking first, before coming to conclusions.

Group Thinking Often Clouds Truth

Do not fall into group-thinking traps. Many people used to think that the earth was flat and that if one traveled too close to the edge, they would fall and die. Group thinking can be fatal because it is the average thinking of people who often conform, a mix of people who think a lot, never think, or sometimes think. Whose thoughts will decide the outcome of your life?

Your Thoughts Create Your Reality

Healthier thinking has made me into a better version of myself. Why live life maintaining the status quo? Life is too extraordinary to be lived only by others' thinking. Challenge yourself and question the things around you. Is conventional wisdom right about a certain topic? Or is it a myth? Be aware when you fall into a group-thinking mentality. Often what helps me avoid siding with the masses is going on a media diet. Be very selective whom you let into your brain. What programs on TV, if you watch often, elevate, and which create fear, or worse, keep you "entertained" with empty calories and in a state of nonaction. Watch wisely.

Morning Thoughts

Today is going to be a good, good day! I believe it and I feel it—say this out loud in the morning to set your day up for success. It is amazing how when I implement this in the morning, before rushing out the door, my day truly becomes spectacular. I gave my mind the command to focus and expect only the best for the rest of the day. Even if things go slightly wrong, I will be able to tweak it into something positive. My mind listens and delivers. It scans the environment all day to find those good things. Powerful stuff. Try it.

Lateral Thinking

I found out about lateral thinking when I was in my twenties when reading the books of Edward de Bono. Check him out. He is an original thought leader. *Lateral thinking* is a state of thinking where you approach things differently. Instead of searching for the obvious answer, you turn your thinking upside down, one hundred and eighty degrees, and come up with something different, something more creative. Instead of thinking A, think M. Instead of thinking red, think purple. Lateral thinking is creative thinking on steroids. It is fun and effective. It is about solving problems using an indirect and creative approach via reasoning that is not immediately obvious.

Thinking Sessions

If you need time to focus on better thinking for yourself, schedule thinking sessions. *Thinking sessions* are like your own therapy sessions, but in your head. Dedicate an hour or a half hour for thinking only, and sprinkle your thoughts with scenarios, ideas, love, questions, spontaneity, and enthusiasm. This is also a time to think about what you want and find focus in your life. Guide your thoughts toward your truth, and you will flourish! I often do thinking sessions in inspiring places. But I also have them in my car; at home; while walking, running, or in the park; while dancing; with or without music; in bed; or when getting a relaxing massage. See thinking sessions as an effective way to exercise your mind, but instead of it being physical, it is mental. This exercise can be life changing. What will these sessions bring? One of the most exciting things: ideas.

Ideas

A ton of ideas will pour out from thinking sessions. Ideas are the Holy Grail. Ideas can change your life in an instant. Ideas can propel you to a heightened state. Ideas are the children of your imagination. The right ideas will give birth to excellence. The right ideas help you and the people around you. Ideas are what caused us to visit the moon, create the Internet, and change our lives from mundane to extraordinary.

Ideas are like little ships arriving on the horizon to take us to amazing lands. Ideas will exponentially help you. Write your ideas down. It does not matter how crazy they sound. Keep creating them, and they will become better and real entities.

> Write golden thoughts and magical ideas down.

When golden thoughts appear, you have to write them down. Do it in the note section of your phone or on a piece of paper. You will forget them otherwise. Discipline yourself to write them in that moment.

Not only will you not forget, but you also can go back and find valuable information. Have a notepad next to your bed and write your ideas down. Ideas do not happen spontaneously. They take years to form through the help of millions of brain synapses. Jot your ideas down so they become tangible things. Trust me, there are things I haven't written down, and I regretted it later. Or the idea came back but took another five years. Why waste precious years?

The Good Old Shower
Taking a long shower while thinking deeply is a powerful way to get to a state of honest truth. Sometimes I just take a long shower to focus my thinking and let ideas come to me. There is something magical when water drops on your body, soothes you, calms you down, and peacefully flows away. Taking showers brings you fully in the now. It brings you into full presence mode, which to me is the same as experiencing pure bliss.

Einstein said, "Why do I get my best ideas in the shower?"

Find the Stoic in You
Stoics turn every obstacle into an opportunity. Feel stoic about the things that happen that you have no control over. Let go of defeating thoughts as if the end of the world is near. Kick doom thinkers out of your life! You will have a better life. Everything will work out. It always does. It is all perception, so you might as well look at it with a stoic mindset.

> Stoics see all that happens as a gift.

Stoics do not get discouraged by temporary defeat; they practice for defeat during better times so they can better face it when it happens. Be stoic about your thinking, and you will free yourself up. My favorite book about stoicism is *Meditations* by Marcus Aurelius. There are different translations, but the one I love, because it is direct and less wordy, is the one from Gregory Hays.

Good Night's Sleep

A good night's sleep can do wonders for your thinking. When I get up in the morning after a good night's sleep, I have a good day. My thinking is stress-free. When you are stressed, you will not come up with the best actions to take. Make proper sleep a non-negotiable thing in life.

> Good sleep is equal to a good life.

For a good night's sleep, I go to bed early. I try not to feel overly emotional before bedtime either. I sleep in a cold room and write everything down I want to do the next day, so it doesn't linger in my brain and keep me up. An important thing I recently started doing is turning my phone off.

When My Thinking Was on Fire

Following your passions and heart will not only make you happier, but it will also help focus your thinking. My thinking became more focused when I moved to Hollywood to become an actress, when I decided to write my first book, when I started my first company, and when I let go of jobs I hated.

My brain is also on fire when I meet big thinkers, individuals who think differently and take me on their fierce journeys. Therefore, it is important to surround yourself with quality thinkers, so they will show you how to push it up a notch. Being around big thinkers makes me feel as if I, too, can fly. Elevate yourself by finding these types of thinkers, and feel inspired.

Positive Versus Negative Thinking Exercise

Let us analyze a simple situation where we could think positively or negatively. What happens if you hold a positive umbrella up in life, and what happens if you hold a negative umbrella up? The scenario is this: It is raining outside, and you were going to picnic in the park with your best friend that you have not seen for a while.

Here is your reaction with the negative umbrella: "Why is this always happening to me? Why are the weather gods not nicer to me? I have not seen my friend for months. Why oh why does it have to rain today of all days?" Tomorrow will be full of sunshine, but neither you nor your friend is available. You react with your emotions instead of thinking with positive intentions, and you cancel the meetup. It will take weeks before you see her again, because you are leaving town soon.

Here is your reaction with the positive umbrella: "It is raining, so what? I am meeting my friend that I miss seeing. I love being with her. Rain or shine, her presence, love, and enthusiasm brighten my day and will take the rain away, and besides, we need the rain because rain gives us life." Take an umbrella with you to cover the food, and have a great time.

We have many options in life, but we often give in to our negative thoughts first. I want you to have an abundant mindset. Wealth is all around you. Tilt toward the positive instead of the negative. You get more done and get closer to fulfilling your dreams. Kick bullshit thinking out of your mind. It clogs your brain up.

CHAPTER 6:

NO DEBT

IT TAKES AS MUCH IMAGINATION TO CREATE DEBT AS TO CREATE INCOME.
—Leonard Orr

I received what many would see as a blessing several years ago. I booked an acting job. They needed a Dutch-speaking actress to fly to the Netherlands, where I grew up, on my birthday, of all days, for a gig that would take a few hours of my time but would let me stay there for a week. Sweet! I should have been overjoyed!

However, I was scared as hell. I had defaulted on a loan in the Netherlands and was afraid that my arrival would trigger the banking system. I imagined landing, walking out of the plane, and hearing a loudspeaker and police siren blaring, as if to inform everybody I had landed.

"There she is!" the angry debt collectors would scream, and proceed to arrest me with handcuffs on my tiny wrists. "Do not let her escape! This bad woman is overdue on her loan payments!"

The loan sharks would march like soldiers, in a

perfect line, ready to guide me to the closest prison so my co-actors would find out what a loser I was.

Luckily nothing happened at the airport. My loan was small, not for me, but for them. They had bigger fish to fry. Millions had defaulted on debt, and even countries had gone bust in recessions. My debt made me feel incompetent. The recession had stifled me, broken my soul into pieces, and lowered my spirit.

I was barely scraping by. Almost in my forties, I still had thousands of dollars in debt *and* debt I had defaulted on in a country I was about to visit for a cool acting gig. I was not in great shape financially. This situation forced me to change and become debt-free. I had to get out of debt to live a meaningful life.

....
To have wealth you must get rid of debt.
....

You especially need to get rid of high-interest credit cards. Avoid them like the plague. Keep one for booking hotels and other expenses, but make it a goal to get rid of this foul plastic.

Every time you take your card out, ask yourself, "Do I really want to pay for this with my credit card, pay high interest, jack up my debt, feel more financial stress, and not be able to save or spend this on worthier events?"

> Living debt-free gives you a better life.
> Pay yourself money instead of giving it to credit card firms, banks, or others.

Living Within Our Means Is Wise

Learn to live within your means instead of being a slave to goods. This comes down to controlling your urges. Stop buying things you don't need. Do not cover pain with shopping. It is only a temporary bandage. Make it a sport to get things economically. Become resourceful, and money goes further. Have days when you don't spend anything. You will feel empowered. A financially prepared soul is a happy soul.

Jim's Crispy Chicken Sandwich

I knew this person, who we will call Jim. Jim had $3 left in his checking account. He bought a chicken sandwich for $10. His account went in the red for $7. The bank charged him a $35 overdraft fee. Now Jim's account was $42 in the red. He could not pay the amount he was overdrawn within a week, so the bank charged him an extra overdraft fee. Jim had bills that were paid automatically from his account, but no income was coming in. His account kept accumulating overdraft fees of $35 every time an item was posted. Eventually his account balance was − $1,000 and went to the collection agency. The bank and the collection agency both made a lot of money on mafia-like fees, and Jim couldn't pay them. This is a nightmare, people. Do not give your precious money away.

Credit Cards—Look Like Heaven but Become Hell

I came to the United States with no credit cards. In this country, establishing credit is important for getting things done, like renting an apartment or getting a job. I got a credit card relatively fast with a limit of $700, but with a high interest rate. I was not going to use it, so why worry? But you *should* worry. It is hard to have credit cards and not use them. Credit card companies encourage us to use them. Advertising tells us that using them offers a more examined life. Socrates would turn in his grave. Why do many young people, who have not built financial literacy yet, get applications and find themselves trapped in using credit to the max? It is hard enough for adults to cope with credit, let alone when just starting out in life.

Shortly after, I got credit card number two, for emergencies. Then I needed a car to maneuver in this town. The first nine months I survived by taking buses, walking a lot, and receiving occasional rides. I got a car loan, I never missed payments, and I had excellent credit, but then something strange happened. The credit card companies increased the interest rates on my credit cards. I was flabbergasted. How was this possible? How could they increase interest when I paid on time every month? It was in the fine print, but who reads thirty pages of fucking fine print? Not me, and I am sure most of us don't. My previous manageable payments with a "fair" interest rate were now increased to mafia-like rates of thirty percent! Yes, banks can do this. If banks charge more than the mafia, you know there is something wrong. Even I, who had a background in banking, was susceptible, so imagine how easily others get wronged.

Do Not Get Them in the First Place

Do whatever you can to keep credit cards out of your life. If an emergency happens and you have to use them, then pay them off immediately! Look at the end of the year and see how much interest you've paid. I guarantee it is equal to buying a ticket to Europe every few months.

Pay More Than Interest

I was in a vicious cycle. I kept the same debt, because of only paying the interest. That is not empowerment; it is enslavement. I was a struggling actress in LA and had no extra finances to pay anything but the interest. At least that is what I told myself. That is how they keep you trapped, my friends.

> Pay more than just the interest, even if just an extra five bucks. Little by little, the debt will shrink.

"Why not charge your customers only interest?" a person told the bank. "You will be the customer's financial ruler. They will pay for a long time." It was one of the smartest ideas this person came up with, and through his "brilliant" thinking, millions of people only pay interest, instead of paying more to lessen their debt.

Leave Them at Home

Your best strategy is to leave your credit cards at home. Your drawer needs them, and they are well positioned in there. If you have maxed out your credit cards, like many of us have, do whatever you can to lower balances.

At a certain point I had five credit cards with balances, but I prioritized paying them off.

Pay Off the Credit Card with the Smallest Balance First

I recommend paying off the card with the lowest balance first.

If you go with the bigger one, it takes longer before you can celebrate paying one off. There is a jubilant dance you do when you pay off number one. And it is just common sense that a $700 credit card can be paid off faster than a $5,000 one.

Cut That Sucker Up

After paying off credit card number one, celebrate by cutting that sucker into pieces.

That is what I did with that first card. I cut it in

about thirty pieces and wrote on a piece of paper that it was done controlling me. I then closed my account. They always make you afraid that if you close your account, it will ruin your credit, blah, blah, blah. I have closed this account and others after, and my credit score is still over 800, which is considered exceptional.

Pay Off Others

If you pay them off and close them down, you will feel a heavy weight lift off your shoulders. I felt empowered after paying off my first card and continued paying off the next ones. The next credit card was $2,000. It took me almost three years to pay all of it off. But what a relief it is when the balance is zero. When you reach this goal, go ahead and get a glass of champagne. You deserve it! It takes hard work and discipline to reach this goal. I am proud of you. It is hard at first, but what an improvement you will experience in your life. You will feel lighter and happier, and a big weight of worry will go back to the banks instead of stressing you out every month paying off these suckers. Bravo!

Stop Using Them

Credit cards kept me in denial for almost fourteen years. Pay them and breathe the air of freedom again. I now pay with cash and only use my debit card. I have money left to do important things that help create my new life. Imagine your disposable income increasing every month by hundreds of dollars. This is money that went to the big banks before, the ones that got rescued by the government while most of us are still suffering and feel enslaved to these cards. I will say it again because it is that important: make it a goal to get rid of your debt.

Celebrate Your New Disposable Income

You'll have more resources to travel the world, take time off, make art, enjoy life, visit nice restaurants, and save up wisely. Do not give your valuable money away anymore. You need it for yourself. Start seeing credit cards as intruders. They are bad agents. Develop discipline and stop your money from slipping away.

Clear Your Mind, Body, and Spirit from Credit Cards

We can be grateful for all we have. Especially in a country like America, we have an abundance of goods. Do we need that extra bag? Often the purchase is for status seeking, which is a never-ending cycle. Clear yourself spiritually from the urge to keep buying. You will feel more peaceful. Experiences are more important, and often they can be done for free! And if you have to use your credit card, only do it in emergencies, when there is no other way—for instance, in a worldwide pandemic.

Save Your Extra Money

I thought that saving money was not cool, that money needed to be burned. I was wrong! Saving money empowers. It will be there for a rainy day, one that you did not see coming. Our job market fluctuates, so save it up, so you feel confident when a stressful situation happens or when you temporarily lose all your income. I write this from experience because I had a setback. I just paid all my credit cards off, and then I heard from the dentist that I needed an acute gum surgery. What? I never had any fucking problems with my teeth. I am the kind of person who is never afraid of the dentist. I go smiling into their office and never have cavities. Now I fucking needed an operation, and my gum was going to be burned away. I had to use my credit cards again because I did not have that extra $8,000 buffer. So please listen to me when I tell you to fucking floss your teeth so you get to keep those Benjamins instead of giving them to your dentist and being on a liquid diet and antibiotics for two weeks. Save extra money so you can take time off to reflect on your life and not have to work nonstop for years. Save money so you can relax. Save that money to build your dreams!

Lower Interest Rates for Cards

As soon as you start paying off your cards and your balance gets lower, contact the bank and ask for a lower interest rate. It makes no sense to still pay high interest rates when you are on track paying the credit cards off. Demand a lower rate. Call your bank up and tell them that you have paid a substantial amount of your credit card debt and showed your commitment to lowering your debt; therefore, you should get a lower interest rate. Threaten them that you will go to another bank if they do not lower your high interest rate. Hopefully they will lower your rate because they want to keep a loyal customer. I cannot explain the change you will experience when you make your last payment. You will become another person. You feel like you are in control again instead of feeling financial terror.

They Are Like a Bad Ex—Exes Should Stay Exes!

There is a reason we broke up with our exes. See credit cards as the annoying ex. Being debt-free is an ecstatic feeling. You experience growth because now you are free from fear and guilt and no longer carry the heavy weight of card balances with you. Credit cards are the biggest bullshit ever made. I can't wait to see you cut that last motherfucker into thirty pieces or more.

Send me a picture.

CHAPTER 7:

RELEASE YOUR ANGER

ANYBODY CAN BECOME ANGRY—THAT IS EASY, BUT TO BE ANGRY WITH THE RIGHT PERSON AND TO THE RIGHT DEGREE AND AT THE RIGHT TIME AND FOR THE RIGHT PURPOSE, AND IN THE RIGHT WAY—THAT IS NOT WITHIN EVERYBODY'S POWER AND IS NOT EASY.

—Aristotle

Most of us have dealt with excess anger at some point; it's a challenging emotion. Anger is powerful, but you don't want it to control you. Anger can help you incorporate change, but do not let it become a full-on destroyer that hurts everything from the little plant on the street to your heart. It will keep you from flourishing and hold you back from becoming your best self.

I am extremely loyal. If I befriend you, you are stuck with me for the rest of your life. If I become your customer, then I will stay, because loyalty is appealing to me. I went through an unpleasant experience with a bank I banked with for seventeen years. I have been depositing checks for years from a particular company I freelance for. It is all recorded, and the bank could see that the check I deposited from this company was not fraudulent. I deposited checks from this company for five years in person or at the ATM. I never had any issues. Then one night all the ATMs were broken, and I wanted to deposit funds to my account. I decided to download their app and do the deposit from home. Initially all was great. It would take two days to clear, and I would be able to access my funds. To my surprise and horror, they blocked the check from clearing for thirteen days! A hold was placed for thirteen freaking long days, just before rent was due and lots of bills needed to be paid. I called the bank three times and explained in detail that I had never had any problems before with checks from this company and that they could see that I made numerous deposits throughout the years. I was convinced the bank would apologize and make sure my check would be credited soon. Nope! Nothing. I was angry since I needed the funds desperately and thirteen days with only twelve dollars left on my account was stressing me out tremendously. I asked them to have some compassion for my situation. Again, they denied my request, and I was without money for almost two weeks and had to use my credit card that I just paid off and committed never to use again. I was furious, and I felt betrayed by them, but then I realized it was not the bank's fault that I had no financial reserve. As an adult woman I had to have a financial buffer for unexpected things. I released myself from my anger and learned a lesson instead: I needed to have a financial cushion. I still was going to look for a new bank, but I also had to take responsibility.

> Anger is often an emotional reaction to something you need to take action on.

What has been boiling up inside of you for a while that you have not dealt with? A moment came when you got super angry. You were done with a capital D! Your anger revealed that you had tolerated your present situation for too long. You had let it happen, but now the straw had broken the camel's back. You thought, "No more, *no mas*, *pas plus*. I am done with this feeling."

You needed to change, and anger helped you realize that. In my case, it was that I needed to switch banks to a bank I felt more at home with and could trust.

Do Not Rely on Anger as a Constant Tool

For some uses, anger is beneficial. I do not get angry often, or, let me rephrase, I try not to get angry too often. It makes me tired; I sleep poorly, get emotional, and become aggressive; and it does not help me to be like a Zen master. When I get mad, it is a gradually building fire. Then my anger moves mountains, feels like a thunderstorm, and becomes a catalyst to getting things done, often fast. The British poet John Dryden said, "Beware of the fury of a patient man."

Einstein said, "Weak people revenge. Strong people forgive. Intelligent people ignore." That is what I do when somebody makes me angry. I ignore and move on. The person raising their ire must have had a bad day and is taking it out on me. I am in no way committed to staying in someone else's angry bubble. Let that person get rid of their steam while I focus on other things, especially regarding the trivial day-to-day stuff like in traffic, in line at a supermarket, or during family discussions. Let this angry energy flow away, and thank yourself for being wiser.

Anger Can Be a Superpower if Used Well

But sometimes anger is beneficial in the right circumstances. We have different emotions in our toolbox, and anger is one of them. If anger helps you focus and change, then that is fantastic. Imagine if Martin Luther King did not get mad and help start the civil rights movement? We would have a different world now. Martin Luther King peacefully channeled his emotions. He was antiviolence but completely proactive and focused on bringing about change "now." He was not passive, but he also didn't allow his emotions to bring him to violence. I am grateful for the ones who stood up, spoke up, got angry, and used it to help humanity.

> We need angry men and women once in a while to stir things up.

Anger Overpowers Other Emotions

Anger is so powerful that it can overpower or release other emotions, like hurt, sadness, grief, and despair. What happens when you feel angry? Your adrenaline gets high, your heart rate speeds up, and your senses explode. You are in overdrive. You may have fire in your eyes, raise your voice, and make wild gestures. It is hard to calm down, but you must. Focus on your breathing and release this unwanted tension.

What are some good ways to get rid of anger?

Clean Like a Mad Person

I clean my house when angry. I hate cleaning. When I can pay somebody to do this for me, I gladly take those dollar bills out, but when I'm angry, I clean like a wild woman. The way I clean the stoves, the walls, the carpet, and all corners of the kitchen is unheard of. Everything will shine and look like new again. I find all the little corners and dust bunnies like there is no tomorrow. Try cleaning, next time, as a healthy outlet, and you will feel much better. It is better to fight with your kitchen cabinets than to direct your anger toward the person you are mad at. After your cleaning whirlwind, your house will look lovely and you will feel better.

Write an Idea List

When in furious mode, write a list with ideas on how to deal with this situation better next time. Write on this list what eases your anger and actions you can take, except killing your boss or family member, to change your situation for the better. Jokes aside, anger can fuel your innovative capabilities. You are in a state of "now or never." This allows you to come up with solutions for changing your situation. There is no luxury of time. Under immense pressure, great ideas and original thoughts flow because of the emotional charge. You can put that list in a drawer and take it out when needed. I recently thought back about my list. One of the solutions on my list to get rid of anger is to buy beautiful flowers. Their mesmerizing beauty melts my anger away.

> Flowers are magical and never angry! We can learn from them.

Anger Is Often a Substitute Emotion

Maybe you have felt hurt, or fear, or sadness, and the emotion came out as anger. Your list can help you process anger more easily the next time something similar happens. One of my favorite poets and philosophers, Ralph Waldo Emerson, said, "For every minute you remain angry, you give up sixty seconds of peace of mind." Think deeply: What has been happening in your life lately? What emotion has boiled inside that you have not healed? If we do not heal our past pains, then they will come out eventually. And in situations that surprise us.

Get Physical

When I feel extremely angry, I go for a run and feel the wind sweep my anger away. Or you can dance inside your house to release your anger too! Physical activity is an excellent way of channeling anger into something more positive and beneficial. You feel better afterward, and your tension is released. Find a way to transform your unwanted anger into a helpful force.

This Too Shall Pass

Another thing to remember is that this too shall pass. Is this thing you are angry about going to matter in five years? If not, release it and move on with your life. The day is too beautiful to be wasted on little things that make us upset. It is a waste to hold on to negative energy. Tell your mind to release the bad thoughts and move on. Better yet, use this whirlwind of vital energy to work on your precious goals. You will launch as fast as a rocket!

PART 2
HOW TO LIVE BULLSHIT-FREE

CHAPTER 8:

MORE TIME IN NATURE

> LOOK DEEP INTO NATURE, AND THEN YOU WILL
> UNDERSTAND EVERYTHING BETTER.
> —Albert Einstein

Nature is everybody's best friend.

Nature does not discriminate. She does not pull favors. She is blind to the color of your skin, your status, your Porsche, or your beat-up car. Have you seen the wind act differently toward a beggar than a billionaire? Does snow crisp more when walked on by a king than by a peasant? Does the sun shine differently on an emperor than on a homeless person? Nature is the great equalizer. Nature does not bullshit around. It just does her work and kicks ass every day.

Nature Is the Number One Giver in the World

Nature provides food, water, oxygen, shelter, spirituality, ideas, peace, warmth, cold, breezes—I could go on for pages about what she provides, but you get the point. Nature is like our mother. Nurturing is in her blood. Giving is in her kind heart. It is beneficial to visit her often. You can learn from nature things you will not learn in other places. Nature is spiritual; she awakens love and puts it in motion.

....
Nature helps us grow.
....

Nature helped me find myself when I was lost. She showed me that letting go, being patient, and enjoying life instead of rushing are key human pleasures. Nature has revealed to me that everything will work out in times of stress. Everything will fall into place, because that is nature's gift. It is a circle that constantly advances the life cycle. She convinced my heart I could do more than I thought I could. Time in nature is crucial for growth and happiness.

Picking Juicy Apples
My first special encounter with nature was as a young girl. My mom and I discovered apples at an orchard near our home where endless rows of trees were begging to be picked. We found the juiciest apples; they were strong and vibrant green and nurtured my soul. The fruit gave us sustenance. It is a cherished memory from my childhood. Eat delicious fruits from nature, and you will receive the nectar of the gods.

Losing and Finding Her Again

I lost touch with nature, like losing a friend who moved to another country. I had to do adult things: climb a ladder in the corporate world and get degrees to make money. I had books to read, essays to write, tests to take, and other so-called bullshit adult obligations that took time. I had no time for nature. Time observing a tree was nonsense. I had to learn how to sell pension funds and banking products and work hard on my career. I forgot about nature, her loyalty, and her healing powers. I thought I could handle a world without her. Not only was I wrong, but I also became disconnected. I forgot how she delighted me. One day I woke up and started to visit her religiously again. Her giving force came back into my life. She empowered me to reach unimaginable heights. If you have lost her, let this be your call to action to go back to her.

Observation Is Key

Have you gazed at the little purple flower recently? Her colorful petals, slender stem, and leaves that blow effortlessly in the wind. You will witness an explosion of mystery. The pure colors of nature will quiet your busy mind. The more you observe, the more peace you will find in your soul. This little flower will give you superpowers if you pay attention to her instead of rushing through the day.

Otherworldliness

Nature transports us to a state of grace, a state of divinity. Does a Sycamore tree struggle, or just grow? It gives us shelter in a rainstorm and also offers great beauty. Have you seen the zooming bee jump on a flower to pollinate so we can eat? Have you observed the grass blade not giving up despite the strong wind attacking and putting her down? It keeps going. It keeps bending, it keeps improvising, so it comes out stronger for the next wind to visit her.

The Poet Ralph Emerson

Ralph Emerson, in his brilliant essay, "Nature," wrote, "Philosophically considered, the Universe is composed of Nature and the Soul." It is just nature and our souls according to him. Emerson was the founder of transcendentalism. The transcendentalists believed in self-reliance, simplicity, idealism, confidence, intuition, living in the moment, and the importance of nature: "In the wood we return to reason and faith."

Let us go back to the woods often and become whole again.

We Cannot Lie in Nature

In nature, we get the truth if we want it or not. Nature brings us back to our core. We feel our primal animal spirit again because we are not surrounded by a cacophony of material things. In nature, we are whisked away from our complicated lives, our jobs, our family, our friends, and our enemies.

No Nature—No Life

There is no denial of the role of nature in our lives. How long can you live without drinking water? How long can you survive without eating foods that nature provides? Nature is a well-oiled machine. She keeps going, rain or shine. Nature is a spiritual warrior and gives us our dignity back in moments of weakness. The force of her generous rivers and streams gives us strength.

Go into Nature to Find Yourself

Go to nature to become a spiritual being again. Go to nature to find your truth. Go into nature to heal your heart. Go into nature to get rid of your bullshit life and kick ass. Let nature caress your wounds and make you unstoppable. The ancient meaning of *nature* is "birth." Go to nature and get reborn every single time.

Our Communality

We might all be different, or speak different languages, but what we all have in common, rich, poor, tall, short, is nature. Every country has nature. To enter superhuman status, one must spend time in it. I love the national parks. Their mantra is, "Take only pictures, leave only footprints."

Many places in nature have taken my breath away. I keep returning to Sicily, the volcanoes in the Auvergne, the Alps of Switzerland, and the US National Parks. In Sicily you have it all, from the Turkish steps that are brightly white, to sandy beaches. In the middle of France, you have the inactive volcano chains, which are a delight to hike. You will see the sheep roam freely, and feel you are going back in time again. You experience beauty that makes you feel you are in a fairy tale. Then the world has amazing lakes, from the glacial lakes in Switzerland around Interlaken, where you feel like you've won a lottery when visiting, or the magical lake in Guatemala, Lake Atitlan.

Find Your Own Nature
Pick your places and indulge. A day, a week, or even an hour will give you a much-needed reboot. I love going to the beach to listen to the ocean, witness the birds that fly around like mini planes, and gaze upon the shells that are glittering in the sun. It is amazing how many colors, sizes, and forms of shells are out there. Do they know how special they are? Probably not, because if they did, they would not let humans trample them to pieces. Visit the beach from time to time. Make fewer visits to artificial shopping malls, and more to sandy beaches. This is good for your wallet too! You can rent a bike and ride along the promenade with the wind in your hair and your legs working those bike steps. They get tanned and toned organically.

Hiking Is Fun and Free!

John Muir said, "In every walk with nature one receives far more than they seek." Isn't that true? Take a hike. Hiking is an easier form of exercising than running.

Sign up for a hiking group. Or hike with a friend. Reach out and offer to take them on a special hike. They will love it, and you both will get to see each other again.

> Go into nature to become connected to your divine source.

Hike the mountains and feel the childlike wonder you've lost. If you invest in a good pair of hiking boots make sure the size is right. Don't do what I did: go to a toe doctor and pay him too much money because you bought a size too small. Go to a specialty store. Do not buy the boots online. Let people in the outdoor stores help you.

CHAPTER 9:

SOLO TRAVEL

I ENCOURAGE YOU TO GO ON AN ADVENTURE WITH YOURSELF. IT MAKES YOU STRONGER, HEALTHIER, HAPPIER, AND FEARLESS. AHA MOMENTS OCCUR AND PUT A HAPPINESS STAMP ON YOUR HEART FOREVER.

—Tania Damha

Solo travel is empowering and nourishing. It opens your heart and mind to different cultures, people, foods, customs, environments, and ideas. It takes you out of your comfort zone and gets you out of a rut. You rely on your own strengths and often increase stamina in the process. The inspiration gained through solo travel gave me a new appreciation of life. It gave me wings. It brought me back to myself. It helped me get rid of my bullshit.

You can always travel with friends or family but increase your superhuman abilities through solo traveling. You build massive confidence while traveling solo and feel more alive. You make new friends faster, feel elevated, and experience pure joy.

Solo travel is a good way to learn things about yourself, things you did not know before. The setup of another country is usually not comfortable for non-locals. You have to learn new customs, habits, and rules. Day-to-day life in other countries is often different from your own. You stop doing things automatically.

> Spontaneity will be your new friend.

Decision-Making

Often we do not make decisions quickly enough in our day-to-day lives. We let them slide, we postpone or ignore them, but when traveling solo, you often need to make decisions on the spot. If you don't, you might find yourself in trouble. Making decisions in the moment is liberating and empowering. If you're not on the ball, you'll miss out on that last bus or train ride to the hotel. If you move too slowly, you'll miss a beautiful sunset or sunrise. If you wait too long to book a cheaper ticket, you might pay more than $1,000 for a ticket to Europe, when somebody else paid $500 and got it during the high season. Most of my flights to Europe have been around $500. It is a great feeling, this lower expense, because it allows you to spend money on other meaningful things.

Uncomfortable First but Adventure Later

Solo travel takes you out of your comfort zone, but soon the unfamiliar will seem familiar. You are more forgiving of yourself because you are on the road. You can keep your own pace. Sometimes you find yourself, sometimes you lose yourself, and sometimes you experience both. Some experiences will blow your mind, some experiences will make you rethink your life, and other experiences will change you forever. I learned to worry less and enjoy the precious moments instead. Great ideas happen in unfamiliar territories, so go find these places in our fantastic and spacious world. Go and kick ass in interesting places in the universe!

Sometimes a Break Is Needed

I started solo traveling when I separated from my husband and decided to take a break from my acting career. When you are an actress in Hollywood, not famous or financially successful yet, and still building a career, you have to go to tons of different auditions. Your agents send you out to meet casting directors, who preselect actors for directors. Agents do not want you to sign out often. If you leave often, they lose out on potential money. When I acted, I hardly took vacations. First of all, I did not have the financial resources, and second, I did not want to upset my agents by leaving often. I only traveled on special occasions, like when my ex wanted to run the marathon in Hawaii. Eventually, though, I realized I needed to do something for myself, so I decided to take a break and travel to find myself again.

Pick a Good City

The first place I went to alone was Paris. If you have never done solo traveling, I recommend choosing a place like Paris, where you can do many things on your own. Visit the museums, eat the delicious and mouthwatering Parisian desserts, some of the best in the world, take a stroll near the Seine. Paris is ideal for solo travelers, and you might meet interesting people. I am editing this chapter in Paris now.

Find something that interests you and go to a gathering about it in another country. It could be a cooking class, a tour in a museum, or a historical walk. It will be a different experience and might help you practice speaking a foreign language. A gathering at home is easy, but going to another country with foreigners is a way to truly expand yourself. I still keep friendships with people I met on my first solo trip. You are in for a treat if you are open to doing this.

Hesitancy to Go Solo

If you're feeling hesitant about solo travel, you're not alone. Some are afraid of not knowing the language, some feel shy, and others are worried about finances. Often shyness goes away while solo traveling. You can learn a new language if you are passionate about conquering it. Or you can do a language trip and attend school abroad. Trust me, you will be fine. The universal language of signs is often enough. Hands, smiles, and nods can create miracles in communication. You will make yourself understandable.

Financial Travel Relief

Traveling doesn't have to be costly. The key is to approach travel differently than the common wisdom says. I travel economically. The reason I travel two or three times a year around the world is because I do it thriftily. I save money on things others pay full price for. Resourcefulness is what you need most in these situations.

It Starts at Home

If you're feeling economically stressed, try a mindset shift: Stop shopping for nonessential things, especially the unnecessary stuff that is not fulfilling, and spend your money on experiences. Stuff breaks down, is thrown away, gets outdated, or loses usefulness, but experiences stay for a lifetime. They are memorable and will be cherished for an infinite time. You relive them and smile and re-experience them again and again. You feel happy when you think back on your travel adventures. If I feel down, I think back on places I visited. I contemplate the grandness, beauty, and newness of places I visited. It grounds me and takes away ugly thoughts. Stuff can never bring the same satisfaction as seeing something as majestic as the Duomo in Florence for the first time, or the power of the Yosemite waterfalls, or the Alhambra in Granada, or the Monument Valley, a spiritual place where the Navajo Indians live. I feel like a little tiny fly when I see this greatness appear.

Experiences are divine. When I missed the regular

bus in Mexico and had to take a chicken bus to Belize City after being awake for thirty-six hours, I had an adventure and saved money. This bus was about to fall apart, with cables hanging out of a box, but all the locals took it. During the day this bus transported chickens. In the evening it transported humans. It was three dollars and took me five hours further. That was a deal I could not pass up. Experiences win over products every single time!

Experiences are unforgettable and special.

Create Disposable Money

Be on the lookout for special airline tickets. Often the obvious strategies are not the best to take. For example, I often visit Amsterdam, in the Netherlands, because I lived there. The obvious thing would be to fly into Schiphol Airport, but instead of flying there, I choose another country to fly into, especially if it is hundreds of dollars cheaper! I fly to Paris instead of Amsterdam and then take the train. If you book the Thalys train on time, you get a one-way ticket for thirty bucks. Book on time when cheaper tickets are still around and spend your saved money on the delicious desserts in Paris instead. Sometimes you can buy night train tickets. You will then save a night in a hotel. Go to sleep and then wake up in an exciting new place in the morning.

Flying Inside a Country

Once I was looking for a ticket to Florence from Amsterdam. Everybody should go to Florence at least once. I recommend going more often. What an amazing city it is. The Renaissance city of the world, where excellence breathes everywhere around you. When I searched, a ticket was $300 from Amsterdam to Florence, but a ticket to the city of Pisa, an hour away by train, was $50. I booked to Pisa instead and took the train for $10 to Florence. Win, win, and win. Not only was it much cheaper to fly into Pisa, but I also saw the beautiful Tuscany landscape. Not a bad environment to see, let me tell you. Question every time if you need to fly into the main airport. Look on a map and see if other carriers fly to a city close by for cheaper.

Days of Flying in and Out

Traveling on holidays can save you lots of money. I traveled on January 1 and got a great deal. Nobody was flying, because they were recovering from a night of partying. A great way to start your year, flying high! What else could you want? You can also grab amazing deals on other holidays. I left on December 31 to Spain almost for free. It was a great feeling because I chased the New Year with me all night long. I arrived on January 1 and had one of the best years of my life. The only disadvantage of flying on a day like December 31 is that you could be dealing with delays. If you have a connecting flight, schedule extra time for changing planes.

Location, Location, Location!

I stay in the center of town, or very near it. You might save if staying further away, but if you have to spend extra on transportation costs, it is not worth it. It also might keep you from going out at night. Especially if it's late and cold outside, you might stay in instead of venturing out. That is a waste of valuable time. I often use last-minute sites to book a hotel. Some will not tell where the hotel is until after you make the reservation. That is the price you pay for getting it cheaper. Others pay full prices, because they want to know the exact name of the hotel.

I think it is exciting to find out later that you got a $300 per night hotel for $100. When searching on these sites, do not only look at the lower prices; also look at review scores for the location. Imagine booking a room, based on price, and then the hotel is on the top of a gigantic mountain and you have to walk with your heavy suitcase, in the blasting sun or late at night. You'd curse yourself or take a cab, which is not always possible.

Start with one night, and then if you like the place, go to the lobby and ask for an extra night for the same or a lower rate.

Flexibility Increases Savings

If you are flexible with travel dates, you can pinpoint dates when major museums or other attractions are free. For instance, in Paris, the well-known Musée d'Orsay is free on the first Sunday of the month. If you book your flight before Sunday, you save on museum fees. Do a little prep work before reserving your flight date. Find out when the good freebees happen in a city.

I go on trips for at least two weeks. It gives me enough time to experience a country. I travel with a small suitcase—especially important for walking up stairs! If you travel in an adventurous way, like sometimes in the morning I do not know where I will end up in the evening, you want to travel light. I love the excitement of sometimes not knowing. It's more spontaneous.

Supermarkets Are Your New Friends

I cannot eat out every night at restaurants, so I visit supermarkets to save money. I love walking the aisles of foreign supermarkets and seeing the different products displayed on the shelves. A good supermarket can be like a candy store for adults. It takes time to decipher the different packaging and what it means, or what it even is, but that adds to the fun. Find the best ones in town!

Visit Outdoor Markets

Outdoor markets are fun, cheap, and good! Experience where locals go and save money. I love big outdoor markets in foreign countries: the noises, the excitement in the air, and the smell of cooked foods, the bursting vitamin-rich fresh fruits and vegetables. I want to bite into every electrifying unknown fruit that lies out there. How would it taste? Is it juicy? Is it sweeter than what I've tasted before? Do I want more of it tonight, and should I buy extra now? Ha-ha! I love fruits, as you can read. You often get cheaper produce at outdoor markets than at supermarkets. Make it a habit to go where the locals shop. You will find unique foods. I always research the daily markets in every place I visit beforehand. This will help you not miss out and maximize your time.

Chat with Cops, Cab Drivers, and Locals

Another tip that will help you choose great restaurants when you do eat out is to ask cops and taxi drivers where they eat. They know the city well, so they are used to people asking for directions, but I ask them where their favorite restaurants are. Ask them not to send you to the typical tourist places. You overpay most of the time, and they are rarely exceptional. You want to experience where the locals eat with families and friends. I have gotten great suggestions throughout the years.

Manage Stress Wisely

It is crucial to manage stress wisely during your travels. Things will go wrong. Even a super organized person like me encounters surprises. Like when I took the train from Bologna to Verona to see Juliette's balcony from *Romeo and Juliet*. I stood at the train station waiting for the train, and it did not come. It turned out I was waiting at 4 Centrale and there was a 4

Este (East) on the other side where I needed to be! Who would think that? Or booking a wrong travel date because during refreshing the website it jumped to today's date instead of the date of travel. Luckily Italians are flexible and helpful with changing train tickets. *Grazie mille*! Manage travel stress by letting go of wanting to have things always go perfectly.

Give it some space. Look at the bigger picture. You want to have a happy, exciting trip, and a few inconveniences are a sign of life. Nothing goes perfectly 100 percent of the time. So breathe, release, and travel on!

I can't wait to hear your travel stories!

CHAPTER 10:

FOCUS IS YOUR BEST FRIEND

IT IS NOT ENOUGH TO BE BUSY; SO ARE THE ANTS. THE QUESTION IS: WHAT ARE WE BUSY ABOUT?
—Henry David Thoreau

Focus is a superpower.

Focused people are powerful people because they get things done. They built the Eiffel Tower, dug the Suez Canal, found cures for polio, wrote books like *The Alchemist*, composed beautiful sonatas, invented electricity, built the first airplane, and kept us away from unnecessary wars. Focused people find their meaning and do not stop till they reach the life they've dreamed about living.

We admire them and want to be like them.

My first experience of focus started when I was six years old. I was an only child at that point. I was happy, loved, adored, got all the attention, and felt like a princess in my perfect world. And then out of the blue two other children arrived; twins showed up in our household, my sister and brother. Up to that point I had full attention from my parents, neighbors, and the whole universe.

But then these two little intruders arrived and shook my precious kingdom, and my perfect world fell like a house of cards. I was in shock. How could my mom and dad see me as invisible where before I was showered with unlimited love?

I experienced pain for the first time. This pain gave me a byproduct: focus.

I realized then that I had to focus on myself. I had to make myself happy and focus on me, instead of feeling jealous and miserable and craving their love, or *only* relying on them for love. It was then, at the prime age of six, that I developed my independence, my own strong will, and my independent thinking.

This strong will has helped me focus numerous times in my life.

Exercise: what was your first experience where you felt focused? Was it through a thought you had or an action you took? What did it do for you? Did you feel pain or love in the process? Did you become stronger? Did it set up the trajectory in your life? Did you stay focused or derail after?

Focus is the most important characteristic to have in a world that wants to kidnap your attention every day. Having focus helps you reach for the stars. Focused people know how to inspire, lead, and help the universe expand. Focused people manage their brain, body, and future well. They have fearless hearts, know what needs to be done, and then proceed to do it, elegantly and swiftly.

Focused people are brilliant humans. They know how crucial this power is to create better lives, for themselves and others. Our society is set up to deprive us of focus. The focused ones live a robust life. They are the warriors, the doers, the brave, and the winners. I want you to join them and understand how important focus is for an optimal life. Focused people know when something is bullshit and run away from it like it is the devil.

Avoid Multitasking Like the Plague

There are several ways to be focused, and multitasking is not one of them. *Multitasking* is not a word you want around. Multitasking causes delay. You think you do more, but in the end, you are less efficient. You do things half-baked instead of fully. There is a beautiful energy that comes with total focus. You can almost taste it. You become an energy beam that goes through the toughest wall, figuratively bends steel, and creates opportunities the nonfocused never get to experience. No focus or not enough of it means no growth, endless stagnation, not finding your destiny, wasting years in a low-end job or years in a high-paying one that takes your soul away, without giving the world your gift it desperately needs.

> Do one thing at a time and do it well.

Focus Brings You to You

The world needs that special talent you have inside but have not revealed yet. I am impressed when I meet people with a high level of focus. They are magical, they are fun, they are full of life, and they have a special energy bursting out of their eyes. They know what they want and go after it. The fire of dedication burns mightily and spreads around. They do not care about going to fancy parties. They do not care to be cool. They want to get shit done, and everything has to go that is not helping them progress. They let go of a feeling of being left out. FOMO (fear of missing out) is strange to them. Focus is more rewarding than getting drunk; instead, they work on their precious goals and reach them.

Like Little Chickens Running Loose

The unfocused walk with faces in their phones and bump into other people or objects, or drive around without looking who is walking in front of them, causing near accidents. These are the people who go from website to website in seconds instead of taking time to read, the ones that take many pictures on a vacation, but if you ask what they saw, they cannot answer you. They took pictures just for the sake of taking them. I want you to develop focus to such a high degree that you find joy as a result. Focus brings you the big prize money!

Unsubscribe

This is a tip I received from a friend years ago. I always choose one favorite word per calendar year, a word that I repeat, think about regularly, and keep around me like a good luck charm. A word that leads me through, reminds me where I am with my mindset, and sets the tone. This year it is *winning*, last year it was *clarity*, and the year before it was *unsubscribe*.

This word, *unsubscribe*, is my golden tip for you. Find a way to implement *unsubscribe* as an action verb in your life. Unsubscribe the hell out of everything that is not serving you and takes precious focus away. Three years ago, I started unsubscribing from everything that did not serve me. My inbox is empty most of the time. Unsubscribe from deals, once-in-a-lifetime events you need to attend, shops that send emails when you bought an item there once, notifications from Facebook, Instagram, dating sites, and others. If you need to find out something, go directly to the page instead of getting annoying notifications all day. These companies are focused on creating notifications for their sales; you should not be. Focus is needed so you can kick ass. It allows you to do everything you want. Implement sharp focus—otherwise you go nowhere or worse, keep living that bullshit life.

Drop Other Projects Now

I started several businesses and owned several websites for companies I planned on starting in the future.

Examples include The Honest Bank, The Honest Cake, Honest Candy, The Honest Drink, The Honest Gourmet, Sanbusak, Magatania, MagaFashion, Special People Conference, Epic LA, IoT LA, and many more. I was all over the place and wanted it all. I think looking back that it was an example of FOMO. This sometimes happens when you are in fear mode and are all over the place and hold on desperately. This is wrong thinking on many levels. If you are spreading yourself too thin, you will only give a little love, effort, and time on each of the projects. I am an aspiring polymath and I love doing different things, but it is better to finish one project first and then move to the next one later. I ended up shutting all of the websites down to focus on writing my book.

Find the Right Environment

Sometimes it is hard to focus in the environment we are in. The barking dog in my apartment complex drives me nuts. I realized I had to change my environment so I could write my first book. When my setting was not serving me, I decided to find that perfect place. My first book is about Happio, a young entertainer in 1930s Spain. He lived in Andalusia in the south of Spain. I thought, "What the heck! I am going to make this happen. I will fly to Spain with my saved-up mileage and go find my character." I booked a flight on Dec. 31 and arrived in Spain on Jan. 1 ready to give birth to my beloved Happio. I traveled in a bus to Granada, and when I got out at the first place, while standing under a tree, a bird pooped on me. There are not many superstitious things I believe in, but getting pooped on by a Spanish bird on January 1, under a tree, is definitely one of them. Winning! Bird poop brings good luck! I knew then that I would be successful and be able to write my book in Andalusia. I wrote more in those two weeks in Spain than in five years in Los Angeles.

Thank you, little bird. Your drops gave me wings!

Find your place where you can work and put your ideas on paper. Another thing you can do is to check yourself into a hotel and work there. Find one where you can sleep well, rest, and write. Trust me, it will be money well spent. Get out of a mundane environment that irritates, so at least you can make a good start. When you get going, you can work on your project at home. I always get a lot done in hotels. The silence, the non-familiar environment, the not having to clean up, and the creative environment inspire me to do more.

Music You Boogied to as a Kiddo

Music helps me to get focused. Certain songs elevate me and bring me into a trance, and in this mindset I am most productive. Music is powerful, and you should be using it as one of your tools. What works well is listening to music from your youth. Ideally, find your favorite tunes from the ages of fifteen to twenty-five. There is something special about this time. You can reawaken the state you were in as a younger person from the songs you loved in the past. Often you remember the lyrics. They will bubble up from your unconscious. Music is an effective tool. You can also dance to the songs and get that body shaking. Do this at home or wherever you feel safe. By listening to music, you might think about lost dreams from your past. It is a wonderful revisit to a time where many of us felt worriless, had not accumulated bills yet, and believed in limitless possibilities. Find those songs and let them take you back to those powerful moments. Another way of letting music bring you into a focused and productive mindset is to listen to one song on repeat. This repetitive listening creates a flow within, and you will create powerful thoughts. What works for me are the songs of Yo-Yo Ma, especially the Silk Road Ensemble series. These songs elevate, sweep me away from procrastination, and help me write—what I love doing and what gives me purpose. Find the right songs that help you focus.

Calm Your Brain

You have to work on your external environment, but also on your internal one.

You need a calm mind so you can focus more. You need to empty yourself so you can come up with golden thoughts. Our mind is often working overtime. We have thousands of thoughts per day, and not all of them are beneficial. You can be distracted by thoughts, such as I have to pick my clothes up at the dry-cleaners, I have to do my wash, I have to buy garlic, I have to throw the milk away, I have to call my friend, and numerous other thoughts.

Exercise: My advice is to write these thoughts down in moments when you need total focus. Then you have a to-do list you can reference later, and you can focus on your task at hand and won't forget about things you need to do.

What Is Distracting You?

What distractions keep you from living your best life? Is it running to the fridge to eat often? Is it endless TV watching? Is it the many times you pick up your phone to check on a new like?

Exercise: What are your favorite distractions? Write a list and then above it with big, bold red letters write, "No more for the next week (or month, or year). So it stops messing with your creative space. When you empty your mind, you create space for golden thoughts to appear.

Where Is Your Blank Sheet of Paper?

Do not wait; take that sheet of paper out or write your list of distractions in the notes section of your phone. Your distractions list will help you finally see what favorite excuses are keeping you from things like writing a brilliant book, moving to Paris, quitting a job you dislike, ending a relationship that is not working, writing that sweet love song, and other things that will lead you to live a bullshit-free and kick-ass life. You can reach that wild dream of yours. It is time, and you got this, but learn to focus first.

CHAPTER 11:

BURN YOUR SHIPS

> WHEN YOUR ARMY HAS CROSSED THE BORDER, YOU SHOULD BURN YOUR BOATS AND BRIDGES, IN ORDER TO MAKE IT CLEAR TO EVERYBODY THAT YOU HAVE NO HANKERING AFTER HOME.
> —Sun Tzu

It was 1485, and a little boy was born, Hernan Cortes in Medellin, a little village in the northern part of the province of Extremadura in Spain. Hernan was sent away to study Latin and law when he was fourteen. His parents dreamed that he would become a successful lawyer, so his future would be one without worry, but Hernan had a different vision. He grew tired and restless and returned home after only studying for two years. Life in a small provincial town was not in the stars for Hernan Cortes.

He heard about Columbus and his adventures to the New World. Columbus became a role model for him, and he copied some of his travels. Cortes went on different conquests and developed into a bold leader, not afraid to take chances. In 1519 Cortes went sailing to Mexico against the orders of then-governor

Diego Velasquez. They had a fight, and the governor revoked his status, but Cortes, brave and unstoppable, went to sail off to far lands anyway. One of the bravest moves Cortes made was in 1519, when he landed in Veracruz to begin his conquest. When he arrived, he gave a nonnegotiable order to his men, "Burn all the ships."

They had to succeed in conquering Mexico, and the only way to do this was to burn their ships to the ground—all the ships they had. Make it drastic, make it final, and make it clear that there was no way back. Burn them down to the ground and do it now. Succeed or die. Do you think Hernan was afraid? Do you think his men were scared? I think they were, but despite their fear, they advanced. Hernan had a strong vision and made his men give up their safety net. All ships were burned to dust. It was the only way to succeed. This is how to progress in your life. Burn them down!

What Ships Must *You* Burn?

What ships do you need to burn so you can proceed in life? What have you been holding onto tightly for days, months, years, or even decades because of fear? What "safe ship" do you live on? What safe ship do you work for? What safe ship are you in a relationship with? Burn those safe ships that give you a cradle to crawl back into and keep you from change. Let go of them with full conviction. You must jump in the unknown and pick the fruits of your bravery.

I Had to Burn Two Ships

I lived in my little studio on Hollywood Boulevard in Los Feliz for seventeen years. The rent was low, the location was very central, and it was in a hip area. I had almost no stress paying rent for years. The low rent was my safe ship—a ship I held desperately onto for years. I did not have to try hard because I could always come up with the rent. What if my rent was triple the amount? Would I have worked harder? Most likely I would have, but this is looking backward. I never will know, but what I do know is that I held on too long to my safe and shitty ship. I should have burned it down a long time ago.

One morning on a run, I saw a big sign posted for a spacious apartment; I knew then that I had to move. I needed more space. My place was small, cold, and lately, not safe anymore—a ship I desperately needed to burn. It had kept me stuck for years. Do not get me wrong, it also helped me for years, but now I needed to move on to bigger and better things. I wanted change badly, and that sign mentioning "spacious" was the nudge I needed. I *desperately* wanted to get out. I'd had enough and deserved to feel good coming home. Moving became my number one obsession. I needed a place that gave me peace of mind, safety, and clarity.

A Deadline Is Necessary

Have a hard deadline. Maybe you do not know an exact month yet, but create a timeline. Write it down and watch those ships keeping you stuck go away. That beautiful big ship you lived on for years, it was safe and risk-free, but not anymore! Tell it, "I am done with you, you piece of shit!" Burn it with full commitment. Burn it proudly. Burn it now. Hernan did it a few hundred years ago. He wanted his men to give it all, empty themselves of excuses, and you will do it now too!

Nothing to Lose

When you take this important step, you start feeling powerful. Your breathing will be deeper. Your shoulders will relax. The look in your eyes will be sharper. You will feel relief. Another ship I had to burn was a mindset change, something I was scared of doing because I had zero experience with it.

I wanted to organize a fundraiser. I had never organized one and had to burn thoughts that I could not do it. I was going to succeed because it was too important. People were dying. It was the right incentive to burn my little "you cannot do this" ship floating around.

Massive Pain in Haiti

A devastating earthquake hit Haiti in 2010. I read an article in the *New York Times* that people were so poor they ate mud. To make it tasty, they added salt to it. I was in shock and pain. How was this possible? How could the world let people eat mud? It hurt my heart, brain, and blood. Who was helping them in this dire situation?

After the news about the earthquake, I searched for fundraisers helping Haiti in the LA area. I was desperate to volunteer. I sought intensively, but to my surprise there was nobody doing anything. In a city with more than four million people, nobody took the initiative to fundraise and stop Haitians from eating mud with salt? I made a fast decision. I had to start a fundraiser myself. But I had zero experience. I had no location, and to be honest, no money either. It was in the midst of a recession. I only had a conviction. I was going to succeed. I had to burn my ship of thinking I could not deliver, my feelings about not knowing how to put an event up in mere days. I also had to rush because people were dying, so I could not plan for months.

Work with What You Have

"Work with what you have" has been a motto in my life. I opened a Facebook page for the event, asking for $20 donations. Friends and strangers shared it. The Facebook page grew fast, and at a certain point had more than a hundred RSVPs on it. With this Facebook page, I was able to ask for sponsorships. I had no idea what I was doing, but I figured if I showed that many people were coming, they would sponsor my event. I was right. I had no track record with fundraising, but people saw my passion. I burned my ships that told me I had no experience. I moved on with full dedication. Luckily the Greek restaurant Papa Cristo's in LA and its nice owner saw my drive and agreed to provide delicious Greek appetizers. Then a friend of a friend on Facebook, Amber, was inspired. Amber has a golden heart and decided to help with sponsorships. I admire her. She is now a successful professional in Los Angeles.

I needed a special location. Through my friend Jennifer Kelly, an events queen in Los Angeles, I was able to get a private club, where normally membership was $2,500 per year. I got this space for free! Yesss! I was stoked. I gave people a cool location, fed them delicious Greek food, and secured a cool DJ that played music and made them boogie.

Find Respected Partnerships

With all this secured in four days with no sleep, I went to the Red Cross. Normally a nonprofit would partner with them, not an individual with no experience. I was obsessed with making them my partner, and they became one. I had to sign a contract that I would give them all the money I collected. As a partner, the Red Cross made my event credible.

I give you this example because this can happen if you make a final decision and do not back down until you succeed.

Let go of limiting beliefs and believe in the success of your endeavors.

You become a pit-bull—so strong, so fierce, so unstoppable that you will break down walls even if you have not found strength yet. Visualize your future happening already. I saw myself with the collected money going to the Red Cross, and as a result of that saw less people eating mud with salt.

Make a Decision of Life and Death

Do you come home feeling unhappy? Visualize owning your own house. You just got a check for $1 million, and you will buy your own house. This happened because you decided to burn the ships that were holding you back. Do you see 29¢ in your bank account because that is all that's left after paying rent? Visualize having $2.9 million so you can help others. Do you look at your body and see that the back of your legs are weak with no muscle? Then visualize having the legs of a runner. Look at runners passing by and admire their legs. Observe them, see their muscles, see their strength, observe the muscle from top to bottom, and see their dexterity and how they move. Then look at your legs. And visualize that you also have beautiful and toned legs. Admire your legs and see the muscles come to life. Then give it a deadline. A half year or a year, but commit to a hard deadline.

Are you tired of being lonely? Go on adventures and meet people. Do you want to be a thought leader and inspire others? Then visualize talking to a big group on stage. Empower yourself, get out, and take life by the horns, breathe life in and be happy, fulfilled, and an active member of society.

Make the Decision Today to Burn Your Ships

Not many people do this. They keep talking, overthinking, postponing, and adding excuses. Make the decision of decisions to go for it. Build the bricks of the yellow road you will travel to create your golden city. A place where financial, emotional, and physical stress are things of your past. Make the decision today, and do not let an earthquake, tsunami, or big bang stop you. Let go of all the bullshit and live your best life ever.

The most important decision you have to make is to let go of your fears. Our fears are often not realistic, but we give them lots of credit. We adore our fears and as a result, stay stuck. Let's move to the next chapter, where I take you on a journey on how you can tackle your fear.

CHAPTER 12:

FEEL FEAR AND STILL GO FOR IT

> I LEARNED THAT COURAGE WAS NOT THE ABSENCE
> OF FEAR, BUT THE TRIUMPH OVER IT.
> THE BRAVE MAN IS NOT HE WHO DOES NOT FEEL
> AFRAID, BUT HE WHO CONQUERS THAT FEAR.
> —Nelson Mandela

I was four and a shy girl. The teacher in class pointed at me and said, "I am out of crayons. Can you go to the other class and ask the teacher for crayons?" I was immediately in a heightened state of terror when he asked me this. I could not just go to another class, full of older kids, and ask the teacher for crayons while everybody looked at me. I was an introvert but did not know what it meant then. I froze, hoping he would ask another child. He asked again, with a louder voice and a sterner look. I got out of my chair with a hanging upper body, acting like I could collapse at any given minute. He led me to the door, opened it, and closed it behind me.

This was my first experience with fear. I felt it in every cell of my body. While walking to the other class, a big door appeared before me. My little four-year-old legs shook uncontrollably. The door was the scariest I had ever seen in my young life. I hoped for a miracle. Could I get the crayons elsewhere, so I did not have to go inside? Gigantic doors surrounded me. I had to go in, otherwise the teacher would find me and embarrass me more. I knocked on the door, but my knock was too soft, the sound a mouse would make, not the sound of a committed crayon collector. No response came. My heart beat faster, and more minutes passed. I still had not gotten the crayons. I then stood straight, let out a big sigh, knocked harder, filled with kiddo's confidence, and waited.

The teacher said, "Come in!" I opened the door, looked in horror at the kids staring at me, and asked for crayons. I stood there frozen. It felt like an hour had passed. The teacher walked to the blackboard. I looked at the ground because the silence made me aware of the slowly ticking seconds. Then the teacher gave me the crayons. I thanked him and walked out with my little hands full of sweat.

I had them! I was so happy. I had survived. I did not die. I did not make a fool of myself. I smiled inside, and my little heart jumped and got a taste of working through fear. I rushed back to class and gave the teacher the crayons. He nodded with approval and was happy to have enough crayons to continue teaching.

I went back to my chair and felt a great sense of accomplishment. Looking back, I am grateful for what the teacher did, because it set the tone for how to deal with fear in the following years of my life.

Now I was less afraid to get the other crayons in life.

A Lingering Virus

Fear is like a virus that lingers in your body and damages you as long as you let it. You visit doctors. You want to get rid of this feeling that does not allow you to function in an optimal way. Each doctor gives you a different cure, but you never get healed, so you seek advice from others, and everybody has a different opinion. Only you can cure yourself of this poisonous virus. You can ask around for a lifetime, but you are the fear creator. People comfort and help, but you have to work on you.

Fear feels cozy; you nurture it and do not resist it enough. You let it grow, because you do not quite understand it. You think it is normal, and it stagnates instead of going away. You cry, you complain, you deny, you despair, you feel pain, and you make wrong choices. You keep at this till that awakened moment arrives, when you say to yourself, "ENOUGH!" This is a golden moment. Fear lessens the quality of our lives. Do not let this disease control your life.

Switch Core Beliefs

You can only conquer fears by changing core-limiting beliefs. You have to retrain your brain to think empowering thoughts rather than negative ones. Create newer versions of thinking that are not stained with fear. Unleash sad thoughts you've kept alive. Incorporate new and exciting ideas and plant them in fruitful grounds, so they grow and flourish. Know deep inside that you will be able to handle it. Just start today and tell yourself, "I have had it, and I am going to do something about it!"

Your First Memory of Fear
What was your first memory of fear? What did you do? What was the result? You survived, right? Did you overcome your fear, or did it make you more fearful? Use this memory to help you identify the fears you have presently. Remember, it takes more energy to stay stuck in fear than to overcome your fears. Push yourself through your fear and you'll improve your life.

Fear Can Be Healthy Too
Remember that fear is also necessary. It is a warning, signaling that things aren't quite right. But if we have staggering fear that keeps us from living life, we need to overcome it. How can we make it a bit easier to handle fear? There are several things you can implement.

Change of Physicality
When I stood in front of that big scary door, I changed my physicality. Straightening my body helped me relax and released tension. Change your

posture and your physical stance, and you will feel stronger.

Control Breathing

The right kind of breathing helps relieve anxiety and fear. Correcting your breathing brings comfort. Start counting to slow it down; slowly count, "One, two, three," and again, "One, two, three," till you bring it down to lower levels. When your breathing is calm, you will feel relaxed and have a better idea of how to proceed.

Feel the *Yes* Already

Another effective way to lessen fear is to "feel the yes already." Look the person in his or her eyes, have your question ready, but first hear the "yes" before you've asked your question. Believe they have granted your wish before you've asked. This is a very powerful technique because it changes your physicality and how you ask the question in the first place.

Your tone will be different, your body language will be stronger, and your words will come out easier. You will feel at ease because you got your yes already and will therefore ask your question differently.

I did this exercise several times when I was leading meetup groups. I was meeting with CEOs and founders of companies, and I had to ask them to sponsor my events. I was looking for event spaces, food, drinks, and sometimes a speaker from their company. Before I went in, I played the meeting in my head before it happened. I heard a yes already, clear in my mind, before I asked. You feel less fear when the moment itself happens. I got most of my sponsorships because I did this exercise upfront.

Powerful Eyes

Practice speaking with passion and show it in your eyes. Create power behind your gaze, and imagine it influencing the person granting your wish. Do not keep your eyes low. Your eyes are powerful! Stand straight, look that person in the eyes, and feel your personal power. Your wish will be granted and your fear lessened. The other person will look at you differently because of your passion revealed through your eyes.

Relax Your Jaw

I often experience tension in my jaw when scared. Do exercises to relax your jaw before going into an important meeting. Move it right to left to loosen your muscles. Make little circles and keep your chin up. Do it in opposite directions. The tension will probably not go away completely, but a little relief is better than nothing.

Wear Powerful Clothes

Think about the perfect outfit, an outfit that makes you feel powerful. The right clothes are often pivotal to get the success we desire. Though our insides are important and determine who we are, we are often judged by what we wear. People do not know your beauty inside yet and can only observe your outside. Think about clothes that make you feel free, powerful, sexy, and ready to go into battle if needed. Even if you have to buy something new, do that. Remember that Superman had his cape too. Make that important investment. The right outfit can put you in the right mindset and elevate you.

To illustrate, I once asked a particular CEO for sponsorship. I wore my red dress, went to a party he gave, had my comfortable high heels on and was not taking no for an answer. It worked! Invest in a few items that you can combine into a few outfits. Wear power clothes like Superwoman. What do you think Cleopatra wore the first time she met Caesar?

Research the Heck Out of It

Another technique for softening fear is to research the topic of what you want ahead of time. Knowledge is power! For example, when I decided to move from my place on Hollywood Boulevard, I researched other houses. I asked myself questions: What kind of place did I want to live in? What area did I want to be in? What apartments were free in buildings I liked? Could I stay in touch with building managers and ask them when somebody moved out, before they put it on the market, to let me know first? This research lessened my fear of moving from a place where I was too comfortable. Do research and have fun, and your fear diminishes.

Create Images

You soften fear by creating pictures of your future. Maybe you're dreaming about a new job. Start researching everything on that type of career. Look on LinkedIn and write to people in that field. Start before you are ready. Tell them you are still in another job, but your dream is to become a member of their profession and as a newbie, you would love to ask them a few questions. People love that. When you write a letter or a note to somebody, make it special, make it real, and make it so they love to read it, instead of making it sound like a sales pitch. Give it the right emotion. Have fun with it.

Courage, they say, is not the absence of fear, but the ability to feel it and still proceed. A bit of fear is a good thing. It will not go away completely. I've heard stories from people who still feel anxious about going on stage after performing for years. Tell yourself that it is normal to feel fear. Not feeling fear at all means you are not reaching high enough. Feel fear and do it anyway.

Develop Pre-Excitement

I imagine having dinners with smart and fun people at my big dining table in my new place. I serve tasty cooked dishes and see them smile and delve into the food. I make them happy in my imagination first, so when I do it for real it will be my second time. Develop pre-excitement consistently. See, feel, and hear how it is when you are living that fabulous life.

Timid souls have timid lives. So develop your pre-excitement to the max, and it will lessen your fears!

I Used to Live Here

Another technique to lessen fear of changing your environment is to drive through the area you live in and do the exercise of "I used to live here." See the present moment filled with the future you want. See how you used to live on this street. See past neighbors, how this was the post office you used to go to, the coffee shop where you used to write. Make it crystal clear that you are in the future now, while in your "old" neighborhood. It helps lessen your fear because you have moved on to better things. You finally took control and got out of a shitty neighborhood you outlived a while ago. You found your paradise.

> Remember, the brain does not distinguish between what you visualize and what is real. So, practice it first in your mind, have fun with it, so it becomes less fearful when you take that important step and it finally becomes your reality.

Doing this kind of visualization will help you change your life faster. I drive around and feel gratitude because I decided to move away—nobody was going to stop me this time. Make this story in your head so real that you already believe it before it happens.

What Are You Afraid Of?

What are the specific things you are afraid of? Write them all down. When you put your fears on paper, they are easier to target. Do not limit yourself; in revealing these things, you will find clarity. Clarity is a beautiful thing because it becomes the mirror we see through.

Who Will You Become When Fear Is Gone?

You became your own doctor. You let go of chains that bound you to the wrong life. Start with the small steps: controlling your breathing, improving your posture, feeling the yes already, wearing the right outfits, researching your topic, being okay with the feeling of fear itself, developing pre-excitement, feeling the "I used to live here"—and knowing who you will become when fear is managed.

Know you can tackle fear. You are the boss. Be filled with enthusiasm, so you can thrive and flourish! We need people who've faced fear and gone for it! Let fear get the hell out so you can experience heaven and live the life you were meant to have.

> Remember the sky is *not* the limit. It is just the beginning! Now go!

CHAPTER 13:

SAYING NO

> **THE OLDEST, SHORTEST WORDS—"YES" AND "NO"—ARE THOSE WHICH REQUIRE THE MOST THOUGHT.**
> —Pythagoras

The stronger a no you say to the wrong things, the more of a powerful yes you create for the right things. Saying yes to the wrong stuff depletes you of valuable time, energy, and focus and does not help change your current situation.

Often we want to please others and engage in activities that keep us away from reaching our goals. You have to create time to make drastic changes in your life, and that starts with saying a powerful no to the unnecessary.

> Too many unnecessary yesses are time killers.

The Importance of a No

We often feel guilt, shame, or fear when saying no to the people around us. We care about our friends and family and want to cater to them. It is important and healthy to have good relationships, but sometimes you have to say yes to you.

You must generate time and energy to fulfill your own goals. If you do this, you will be happy and content with the outcome of your life. There is only one life to live. Do you want to waste it on saying yes to distractions?

You are committed to making your life work for you. You've wasted many nights and days and are tired of letting life slip away. Say no more often and create the time to build your dreams.

A no will help shift your priorities. It is often hard to utter this two-letter word, but you can train yourself to do this. With experience comes mastery. If you want to create time to accomplish your dreams and get unstuck from an unhappy life, then you have to say it often.

First, say no to simple little things, until you get comfortable tackling the bigger stuff, like situations where you know the other person will get upset. The more you practice, the easier it becomes. Saying no will not always be easy. You might lose friends, your family might get angry, you might lose a job, you might disappoint people, or you might get kicked out of a group, but what you gain is personal power and time.

> You might lose other people, but you will keep yourself.

You will climb the stairs to your dreams faster. You will find your destiny sooner, because you've dumped distractions. There will always be another party, dinner, or event and more fun to have, but there will not always be momentum, which I imagine you may be feeling at the moment.

Train yourself to say no often, so unwanted situations will not cause you to stagnate. I had a job situation where I had to say no. I wrote advertising copy for online merchants, and I was able to work from home. This was great because it gave me flexibility in my schedule. I worked there for years and always did a great job. Then they wanted me to work in the office again, drive two hours in traffic in the morning, work for a few hours, and then go back home again, spending two more hours in traffic. This was a job where they explicitly looked for people to work from home—that is why I took it in the first place. Then they changed it, voila, without asking us for any input. After beating traffic for two weeks, it felt crazy to make the commute. I spoke up. I said it was not a fair situation. I hoped they understood. They did not. They did not like my no. It was the last time I heard from them.

Good Things Come After a No

Getting dumped by them turned out to be one of the best things that happened in my life. The extra time allowed me to do more important things. If I had committed to staying at the job and said more wrong yesses, the kind that kill dreams, I would still be writing online copy instead of this book. I said no, and my stable yet stagnating job was over, but it helped me gain courage to focus on my writing and pursue my dreams.

Others Not Understanding

There is a chance people will not understand your no. Keep that in mind when you want to say it. Know that this *is* the change you need in your life. Rethink the yesses you say that unconsciously make you miserable. Commit to being okay with being uncomfortable first. Afterward you will experience freedom in your life! Nobody who has done great things was comfortable initially. Accept being scared in the beginning. Feel the burn that you might run out of money while you finish your dream project. Feel the anxiety of losing a side hustle. Sometimes everything has to fall down before it can grow to mind-boggling heights. You finally found your potential and are going at it in full force.

Say No with Conviction

Do not say your no softly because if the person feels your weakness they might convince you to change it into a yes. Say it loud; say it proud and with conviction.

Cater to the desires of your heart by saying more nos. Practice saying empowered yesses to yourself and hop on a launch pad toward your destiny.

How to Say No to a Friend or Boss?

Say no at the *right moment*. When do you say your no? Do you say it in the early morning, when your friend is sleepy (and she is a night owl) or do you say it in the afternoon, when she is awake, and it lands better? Another thing to take into consideration is the *right kind of communication* to whom you're saying a no. If it's a good friend, use a smile, give a hug, and express it with love and care. If it is your boss, then use a different approach. Always use the right kind of tactic. Different people need different styles of communications.

Say It with Tact

When you say no, you have to use tact. If you are saying no to a real friend, the one you can call at 3:00 a.m. and they will pick up because they want to know what is wrong, then just *be honest* with your no. Tell them, "I am on a sacred deadline and want to celebrate when I'm done. Let's go out, eat, drink, and be merry when I have more time. You deserve devoted time instead of me meeting you, rushing, and maybe not being in the right mindset." They will understand if you say it politely. If the person is not a real friend, then the outcome could be different. I've lost a few people when I've said no.

Some people will become jealous, some will not understand your focus, and others will still want to hang on to the old you. They hate seeing you change and skyrocket to your dreams. But you have to move on and do what's right for you. Focus on friends who are there in good and bad times, friends who encourage you to work hard because you've found your purpose. These people want to see you succeed, because it makes you happy. Be selective about who you spend time with; people influence us deeply.

Do Not Say No All the Time

Keep your no to yourself when the greater purpose is served. We live in an interconnected world, and we do not always get what we want. Sometimes you win and sometimes you lose. A no can sometimes disturb the ecosystem. This can be within friendships, at work, or with your family. Imagine your aunt just made you the ugliest sweater in the world. She went to the store and bought yarn in the colors of brown, lime green, and purple. They were on sale, you know, and she paid for them with her little monthly pension. It took her weeks to make you this sweater, because she loves watching soap operas, which take all her time, and she can only knit when they are not on television.

Are you going to say no when she presents her creation with a big smile and crooked teeth? No, you take it and thank her. A little discomfort can at times be helpful, for us and others. Things you think you will not like turn out to be life changing for others.

But if you are reading this, you probably do not like your job or your current situation and want to leave. You must add no to your vocabulary, so you can do the things you love.

> Change your bullshit life into a bonanza!

Put No in a Little Packaging

Be tactful when saying no to superiors, especially your boss. Your no can get you fired. It happened to me but liberated me. If you have to say no to your boss, say it with a little *pre-story*. Put him or her in the right mindset first. You could say something like, "John, I have been working here for a while, I have always come to the client dinners, and I am engaged with my work, but I cannot attend next week's event. I have to say no." This way, your no does not land as hard and comes with a little packaging. This kind of no has, for the most part, created empathy for my cause.

Exercise: Before you move to the next chapter, take a piece of paper and write down all the things you need to say no to from now on. Especially when you are working on a specific project, this exercise can be of tremendous help. Write it down and do not overthink it. What will help you and what will keep you stagnant? Put this list on your desk so you can look at it in moments you need extra empowerment or focus.

CHAPTER 14:
ACCEPT SETBACKS

> SUCCESS CONSISTS OF GOING FROM FAILURE
> TO FAILURE WITHOUT LOSING ENTHUSIASM.
> —Winston Churchill

A swollen knee that felt like an inflexible piece of hardwood; a car mirror that was hit, dangling like a sad puppy's face, $450 to fix, with only $900 left in my bank account to live on for seven more weeks till I would go back to work and make money again. A training schedule I had to stop a few weeks before my marathon in Paris, and three dogs in the apartment building barking like it was the end of the world. It was an eventful morning when I wrote this chapter about accepting setbacks. When setbacks come into your life, they always seem to come in big quantities, like a heavy rainstorm with thousands of drops.

Setbacks Will Come

Even the strongest, most powerful, luckiest, and most focused people will experience setbacks from time to time. With many things in life, it is often not what happens to us, but what we do with what happens. I had my car mirror fixed, and the guy was nice and gave me a 15 percent discount. I rested the knee all night and walked to the coffee shop to write. I gave my knee love instead of messing it up and cancelling the marathon I was training for. Tickets and hotels were booked in Paris. I needed to stay calm, focus, think about solutions, and take action.

Questions to Ask When Setbacks Appear
How do we change setbacks and make them manageable? What do we learn from them? How do we adjust after our setbacks? What is the powerful lesson we are getting? Maybe something we denied doing for months? It is important not to fall into a state of despair. Stay calm and focused. How can you turn your setback around?

Take the Emotions Out
I advise you to take your emotions out of the equation. Desperate emotions lead to desperate actions. We feel anger and emotion bombs go off. We might cry, we might yell, we might be scared. This is all good. Let emotions flow, but as soon as you can, force them to leave so you can think clearly. *Delete the emotions.* Look at your situation without emotion, so you can come up with a better solution. What are your options? What could you do? Whom could you ask for help? What should you stop doing? We get a

clearer picture when we take the emotions out of our situation. I have had several major setbacks in life, but always thought while in them, "What is the lesson here, Tania?"

She Likes It Hot

I think life is hell without a good hot sauce, so I created my own hot sauce company, which I ran for three years. This experience taught me a valuable lesson. The product I made was a unique sauce for the female market. Most hot sauces I purchased were too manly looking. There must be women, I thought, who also love hot sauce but do not want to *only* see a manly label that screams things like, "I am going to kill you," "Burn in hell hot sauce," "Hot sauce that burns tongues away," "Die fast with our hot sauce," or other variations.

I tried a hundred different recipes in my tiny kitchen. I mixed different peppers, ingredients, flavors, and roasted vegetables and got to work. My fridge was full of little glass bottles with different sauces, in different colors and sizes, lined up neatly in a row with the date written on with a Sharpie pen. It was the midst of a recession, and I felt the urge to create something to keep me going; I had unwanted free time due to the lack of work.

My goal was to come up with a luxury hot sauce, one that was not yet on the market. My hot sauce would taste heavenly. Its flavor would make you feel like you'd arrived in a special land, a land I called

Magatania. I came up with the name because *maga* means "sorcerer, magician, and creator." I found a manufacturer, not easy when wanting low production, launched a Kickstarter campaign to get production financed, and found a great designer for my labels. I was thrilled when I picked up my first batch of hot sauce. I had done it—with a few setbacks like finances, not finding the perfect manufacturer, and lots of delays. I was ready to sell this delicious sauce to my fellow hot sauce kings and queens. I had worked years nonstop to make this a reality.

I set up tastings in gourmet stores, supermarkets, and little mom-and-pop stores. I drove to San Francisco where I set up a table and presented my hot sauce on salty crackers. My friend filmed my interaction with the consumers.

I was ready, my hot sauce was ready, and San Francisco was ready. I stood behind my table and served my first customer the Magatania hot sauce on a little cracker. I could not wait till he would say that this was the best hot sauce he ever tasted in his life. Instead, he coughed. Then he coughed harder. And then he coughed even more. He thanked me and rushed the hell out.

More customers came in. The same ritual kept happening. I gave them the hot sauce, they put it in their mouth, their tongue caught on fire, they swallowed it, and they coughed hard. This kept going for hours, throughout my entire tasting. About 80 percent of the people who tried my hot sauce coughed after. "Hmmm," I thought. "What is happening here?" This supermarket is a prominent, hip, super healthy store in San Francisco. The consumers are very health conscious, so I thought to myself, maybe, just maybe, they like more of a bland taste. They are not into a spicy, exotic Moroccan hot sauce, but a version with less heat.

What I needed was to have a tasting at a real hot sauce store. A place where my kind of people came: people who had hotness come out of their mouths and noses and still kept a huge smile on their faces, the Julius Caesars and Napoleons of the hot sauce world, the fierce Cleopatras and Joans of Arc. I scheduled another tasting at a real hot sauce store in Berkeley. People came here specially to buy hot sauce. I set my table up, people sampled the sauce, and again, they coughed. Not as many coughed as in the supermarket, maybe 70 percent, but they still coughed hard.

This was a setback that became a lesson for life: I had not done enough testing in the market. I had only asked my friends, and taste tested them, and guess what, they all *loved* my hot sauce. They are my friends! Whenever you launch a product on the market, do not *only* ask your friends for feedback. You see, sometimes friends will say that something is great because they don't want to hurt us. Sometimes they like similar things. I worked hard and nonstop to put this product on the market and drove around from city to city to make it a success, only to find out after two years that the damn sauce was too hot. We were in the middle of a recession, and all my hopes were resting on this product to generate much-needed income for myself. It did not happen. My spicy sauce was not made for the many tongues out there. I had not thought it out deeply enough, but I had learned a much-needed lesson.

This Setback Was a Huge Lesson

I actually learned more than one lesson from this experience. I had done everything wrong; it was the wrong product on several levels. I had created a gourmet product during a recession, when people don't have gourmet money to spend and look for cheaper products. The sauce was too hot for most people. And it was too expensive. I had chosen the manufacturer because it offered the lowest production units, but this caused the price to be higher per unit.

This experience was a major wakeup call for me, and eventually, I was happy this setback happened. The lessons from my hot sauce fiasco were clear. I realized that I did not want to be the new hot sauce queen in town. I made the product during a recession thinking I could make some easy money in my deeply deprived financial situation. However, I did not want to drive to multiple stores, burning gas, to make deliveries of my sauce for the rest of my life. Sure, I still love hot sauce and will always love it, but it was not my destiny.

I also learned not to ever do a job primarily for

money—you will burn out or lose motivation and be unhappy. If you have to work only for money, because you have no other choice, promise yourself to only do this temporarily. Work should be instilled with purpose, so it keeps you going during challenging times.

This Too Will Pass

When you have a setback, the trick is to see it all as temporary. You will come up with a new solution. The knee will heal, the car can be fixed, and the right idea will show itself. Do not think because of a setback that you will not be successful with other endeavors. Setbacks are the best educators. If you implement the wisdom you learned during your last journey, you gain insight about yourself and your process. Do not let setbacks last longer than needed. Here are techniques that helped me.

Let Humbleness Take Over

Feeling humble can change you from reacting from a place of ego to a place of wanting to learn. Every time I eat my humble pie I become calm and trust that life will lead me where I should be going. Being humble is a cleanser that can wipe out the unnecessary. Let it wash you clean. Feel humbleness deep inside of you and do not push its power away. Then, after finding your answers through being humble, look at what the setback is telling you. Are you really on the right path doing what you are doing now? Is this project you are committing to the best use of your time? Are you doing it to reach your goals, or are you doing it so you don't lose face?

Think About Prevention
Do a deep analysis of your last setback. What did you learn from it, and what lessons can you take from the situation? Was there something missing from your plan? Did you react with too many emotions? Should you have said no to something? Is this the best use of your time on this earth? Asking yourself questions and thoroughly thinking the situation through helps you save time and will give you peace of mind.

What Are the Specific Lessons?
I learned that I had to ask a wider variety of people for advice, even strangers, who are not afraid to say less flattering things. I learned valuable lessons for my next endeavors. For my books, I plan to have them preread before publication, by people in bookstores, random strangers, people on Amazon who write reviews, and a much bigger pool of individuals. What lesson have you learned from one of your setbacks?

Silence the Panic Monster
The next step after a setback is to shut up the panic monster. My panic monster had been silent for months while I was creating the hot sauce. I was focused on my fundraising, driving to the manufacturer, and working with printers for the perfect label.

I had quieted the panic monster that tells me how I suck. With this setback, the panic monster woke up from its sleep. It would say things like, "See, you are not meant to create unique products that can help people," "See, you have too big of goals in life," "See how you suck? You cannot even make a mild hot sauce. What makes you think you can follow your dreams and live your best life ever?"

The panic monster was ready to attack. It had been asleep because I did not give it space while I was busy creating. Every one of us has some version of the panic monster, our negative voice inside that discourages us from taking on worthy goals. You have to silence it after a major setback occurs. It is not the end of the world. Breathe deeply, rest your body, ground yourself, and find the positive around you. Maybe it's time to try something different that will not be so taxing, or maybe new strategies will present themselves after taking a little time to rest and reflect.

Transform Setbacks into Positive Experiences

Remember, after a dark night, there is always a bright morning. New mornings give us new perspectives, wash away darkness, and help us refocus and regroup. This is the yin and yang of life. In everything positive is something negative, and in everything negative is often a silver lining. Setbacks will still come, but do not let them take away your joy or drive.

They Are Mirrors We Have to Face

You have the freedom to choose how to transform a setback into a positive experience and learn valuable lessons. You need to keep going, stay calm, see it as temporary, and find new and exciting solutions. Transforming a setback into something positive is fun and healthy and brings you closer to your dreams.

PART 3:
DEVELOP AN EXCELLENT LIFE

CHAPTER 15:

FORGIVENESS

WHEN YOU FORGIVE, YOU IN NO WAY CHANGE THE PAST—BUT YOU SURE DO CHANGE THE FUTURE.
—Bernard Meltzer

See that donkey walking up the steep hill? There are no cars or freeways around, just a poor donkey puffing hard, climbing up a steep hill in the blasting sun with eight heavy bags hanging on his back. There are four bags on his right and four bags on his left. They give him balance; otherwise, it would be even harder. He is sweating, he is tired, he is in pain, but keeps walking up the steep hill.

He does not know better. He glances up and sees the big green tree appear on his right side. This is the moment when he takes a deep breath and lets out a big sigh. He knows he is getting closer to the top, the place where his present situation will change. A few more steps come up. "You can do it," he tells himself over and over.

Puffff, puffff. He finally arrives at the top.

There is Pedro, an older man with dark red skin.

The sun has burned him deeply over the years and caused his skin to wrinkle. Pedro walks to the donkey and takes the bags from his back. One, two, three, four bags on the right go off, onto the ground. The donkey feels relief in his right shoulder again. The feeling is sublime. He looks up to the sky and smiles. The marks of the bag handles are still showing on his skin. Then one, two, three, four bags on the left drop onto the ground. The donkey looks up again to the sky and is in donkey heaven. He is relieved and makes his usual sound, the sound of a joyful donkey on steroids.

Do Not Be Like the Donkey

A state of not wanting to forgive and carrying unforgiveness around is living the life of the burdened donkey going up hills. You carry the unnecessary with you because you are not ready to let go yet. Living in a state of anger and not wanting to forgive is a state where bags constantly dangle on your shoulders. You are sweating, puffing, and walking in a blazing sun and not realizing why you are still having so much pain in your life. Do not be like the poor donkey.

What Experts Say

Psychologists often define forgiveness as a conscious decision to release feelings of resentment or vengeance toward a person or a group who has harmed them, regardless of whether they deserve to be forgiven. It also does not mean you will forget all they did. Decide to release yourself from your heavy weight. Remember while you move forward that forgiving is *not* forgetting.

Learn to Forgive

Forgiveness lets us unload.

Practice unloading more often. Forgiveness is needed if you want to feel superb in life. Why go through life like the poor donkey carrying heavy bags? They hurt, they are useless, and they make you go slow. They are not needed. Forgiveness gives you back precious energy. The kind of energy you will not waste on anger, always wanting to be right, or following your ego.

Forgive to Rediscover the Real You

Forgiveness is not easy. But implementing this superpower will give you freedom. Remember, we are not asking you to forget. But by forgiving you are taking care of yourself. I know from my own experiences that I had to forgive to become powerful. A few individuals in my life made me angry because of their actions. I carried heavy bags like the donkey. By not wanting to forgive, I was stuck. If I wanted to grow I had to get rid of them. I threw them off.

You Are Not Always Right

Realize that you are not always right. It will help you forgive those who have wronged you. What if you told yourself a story and it turned out to be completely false? Think of situations in the past where you were convinced the other person wanted to hurt you, but instead they were in pain themselves. Maybe they did not contact you because they were going through rough times. Things are not always how they appear. Increase your love and take that first step by forgiving. Do not always assume you know the whole truth. We often have biases that derail us.

Try to Understand the Other Person

Try to understand those who hurt you instead of judging them. It is not always personal. Having empathy helps calm you and gives you the ability to forgive instead of getting mad. Holding on to judgment and anger makes things worse for you and can escalate a situation. Often our interpretation of what happened is incorrect; we are not always right. Heal old pain instead of holding on to it, and as a boomerang it will heal you too. This is powerful stuff. Be the peacemaker and see yourself as a leader who forgives and moves on.

Learn from Mandela

When I think of forgiveness I think about all the great people who came before us and set an excellent example. Just look at Nelson Mandela. In 1990 Nelson Mandela, recently released after twenty years in a South African prison, spoke to a crowd and said, "We especially need to forgive each other, because when you intend to forgive, you heal part of the pain, but when you forgive you heal completely." If he can do it after being in prison for twenty years, his dignity and freedom stolen from him, then we can at least make an effort to do this too.

Release Your Bags
What are some bad feelings you have toward an ex, a family member, a friend, an acquaintance, a coworker, a neighbor, or a random stranger? These negative emotions carry heavy weight around. And it does not feel good. We already carry enough weight in our day-to-day lives. Some of it we cannot change, but what is it that we can change? Which situations should be reconsidered after staying in anger mode too long? At the end you forgive yourself by letting it go.

I went out with a guy and had a great date. It lasted twelve hours! Our second date lasted for fifteen hours! Holiness, this was great! Then he told me he did not feel it. Seriously? You were with me for fifteen hours and then you "do not feel it," dude? I thought of him as another BS guy. Then he kept in touch. I was confused and brushed him off. He persisted and asked to meet again. First I thought, "No!" but I rethought my stern reaction. Forgive and move on.

Return to Yourself
After I forgave people, I felt like myself again. While I still held a grudge, others had moved on with their

lives, and I was still trapped. When the bags lifted, I had a healthier body, a stronger mind, and less on my back. Do it for your sanity; release yourself from this unnecessary pain and gain peace in the process. Experience how it heals you.

CHAPTER 16:

GIVING

NO ONE HAS EVER BECOME POOR BY GIVING.
—Anne Frank

It was a beautiful morning in LA. I washed my clothes, ordered new contact lenses at Costco, ate my juicy orange from the farmer's market, felt the bright sun shining on my rested face, and decided to do some writing. I did not know exactly what to write about yet. Usually the topic comes to me in the morning, and then during my writing session I develop it. But today I had not yet pinpointed it.

Writing had been a habit lately, and I had been frequenting many coffee shops for inspiration, since visiting new places gives me a jolt of ecstasy and boosts my creativity. Today I was at Bourgeois Pig in the heart of Hollywood. Leonard Cohen, the Canadian singer and poet who spread love with his artistry, used to be a regular here. I attentively observed all the objects around me, and my heart beat a little faster in awe. I felt like a little kid in a candy store. There was the comfy couch that a million people had sat on and a hanging disco ball flickering with lights that brought me back to dance parties from my past. The darkness of the place reminded me of a Harry Potter story, and I was transported into a magical world. Someone imagined the interior of the cafe first, before it came to be. I observed and contemplated the creator's vision and was inspired.

I decided to visit more places that were hotbeds for writers, places where the writer's community of Los Angeles wrote and mingled, so I could feel the inspiration lingering in the room.

While walking up to the coffee shop, I saw a woman sitting outside of her house smoking a cigarette. She wore a black winter coat with a hood made of wool, the kind of coat you wear when you travel to Antarctica.

I walked by, surprised, and asked her without thinking too much about it, "Are you cold?"

"No," she said. "I do not like to have my hair smell like smoke." She said it with a grin, and I laughed, and she laughed even harder.

"That makes sense," I replied, and smiled and walked away.

Did it make sense? Of course it did not make any fucking sense. It was eighty degrees outside and too hot to wear an Antarctica coat, and the smoke would go through the hood anyway. But it did not matter. I made her feel good by saying that it made sense. We both laughed about it, and without it being expressed, we both knew that what she said was nonsense, but it did not matter, because it felt good to agree.

At the core of this interaction was the gift of giving.

I wanted to give this woman a good feeling about herself, first by talking to her and second by agreeing with the action she took. Then I realized: I had found my topic to write about for today. I would write about giving!

Giving can come in many different forms. It can be time, money, words of encouragement, a touch, a look, a smile, a handwritten note, a listening ear, a hug, or anything else you do with your heart.

The most successful people in the world are major givers.

You should be a giver. It is a superpower. Do not *only* give to people you know, admire, or want to benefit from. Give to strangers. Give to different kinds of people. It makes them feel good, and it will make you feel even better.

Give Because You Want To

Giving will make you stronger. People who are major givers are fearless. They are not afraid to run out of resources. They believe in abundance and that when they give it will come back to them, or if not, they are okay with that too. The giving is the reward. The heart has spoken, and the mind followed with an action. Giving is bliss. There will be times in the future when you need love back, and the people you gave to generously will often reciprocate and give back to you.

Never See Giving as a Strategy

Never give without meaning it, because the receiver will feel it. Give because your heart wants you to give. I have seen people give with a heart full of fear. It is not a pleasant sight—and fake. Give because there is joy in it. Look at somebody's face when you give that unexpected gift. It does not get better than that. It is an empowering giant. It will come back to you, in different ways than you expect.

Giving Will Enrich Your Life

My earliest example of the power of giving came from my dad when I was five. On Friday mornings, there was a weekly market in Maastricht, the city where I grew up in the Netherlands. My parents went to this market to shop for fresh produce, fruit, fish, and nuts. This particular morning my dad and I went together. We bought oranges, a few kilos of them. We ate a lot of fresh fruit, because in Morocco my grandparents had a big farm with fruits, so we were raised with it. My dad bought oranges and gave the market man ten bucks. He got his change back, and we walked toward the car. It was parked far away, at least a two-mile walk. As we got closer to the car, my dad pulled the change out of his pocket and looked at it. Surprised, he saw that he had received five bucks more than he was supposed to get back.

He told me, "We received five extra."

I responded, "Well, that's great."

I was happy. "Yes, extra money!" Maybe he would give it to me and I could buy candy.

"Very good, Daddy!" I said again.

"No," he responded. "It is not good. We have to go back and give it back."

I tried to discourage my dad from doing this.

"No, Daddy, we need to keep it. We should not go back. It's a long way back."

"No, we have to go back," he said again.

We walked those two miles back and approached the market man. My dad told him that he had given him an extra five bucks. The market man looked surprised. He could not believe it. This type of honesty was rare. I saw as a little kid the power of this situation. He took the money and said, "You have a very honest dad." What my dad did that morning not only made the market man feel good, but also changed me for the rest of my life.

Lives Change Through Giving

I was going to be a giver, too, because of this lesson. You never know what can happen if you give something back that does not belong to you. The market man got the gift of knowing that honesty was still out there in the world. A gift might pull somebody out of a depression, a gift might put somebody back on track, and a gift might give somebody hope.

> We change the world by what we give.

Do Not Keep Track of Giving in a Bookkeeping System

Give without expecting anything to come back, because if you do and it does not come back the way you want it to, it will turn into pain. If you are going to keep track of who gave and when and turn it into a sort of bookkeeping system, you will get disappointed fast. Here are tips on how you can be a giver, with or without money. Money is not always a requisite.

The Most Important Gift Is Your Time

Everything can be bought or replicated, but time cannot. When it is gone, it is gone forever. It is therefore an extremely valuable good. How can you give more of your time? Time is a sublime gift we give to others. It will be cherished for life! Spread time to others to help them. When people see that you make time for them, especially when they know you have a super-busy schedule, you warm their hearts. And by warming their hearts, you give them encouragement and power.

Give your time to your loved ones!

Start Volunteering

What are you passionate about? Who needs help in your community? What field do you want to learn more about? What makes you feel good when you do it? I first volunteered at the Braille Institute in Los Angeles. Because I love the senses, I asked myself which of the senses I would be sad losing. For me the answer was sight. I wanted to help those who had trouble seeing.

The Braille Institute turned out to be only a few miles from where I lived, which was perfect. I walked in and filled out a form, and they let me help the yoga teacher in her class. It felt so good doing this. I felt noble contributing my time and love to people who appreciated me. I thought I was helping them, but their love helped me. I did it as long as I could. The yoga teacher eventually moved back to South America where she was from, and the class stopped, which was unfortunate. It was one of the best experiences in my life. I volunteered after this experience at many other places. Find a place to volunteer and give your time so you can help others. You'll create happy moments for others—and yourself.

Give More Time to Your Friends

The older we get, the more important our friends become. Friends, we get to choose; family, we do not. Make yourself available to them. Do not always say you are too busy; get that word out of your vocabulary, as we all are busy. Time with friends is healing. You will feel good, they will feel good, and the world will feel good.

Give Smiles

Smiles are free. They are delightful magical things and can change somebody in a second.

Give smiles to strangers, to the girl behind the cash register, to the policeman working to find criminals, to the person sitting next to you at the coffee shop, and to others who you encounter daily. Smiles are the gold we carry on our face, so let your brilliant smile not go to waste. Smile, and smile often.

Give Money

If you are hardly surviving, living from paycheck to paycheck, then commit to giving later when you have the resources. Find organizations you are passionate about and help them. Your giving goes to people less fortunate. Especially in Western countries, we have so much and do not even realize it. There are still millions of people around the world who do not have enough money to eat. Imagine you had to live on just one dollar a day? Give the amount you can miss, and let the goodness of your heart help others.

Give the Right Emotions

Instead of getting mad at your family and others, can you give them more of your patience? Instead of bursting into your normal angry state, can you try to understand them instead? Give them the benefit of the doubt. Select the right emotions to give to people. Learn to balance and control them instead of acting out.

Count to Five If You Have to

Give the person who cut you off in traffic a less stern look. You can blow up like a balloon and pull out your middle finger, or just nod and let it go. Emotions fill us and are often in our body for hours. Select them wisely. Do you want to stay upset for a long time in the wrong way? I don't think so. Send the right emotions in your giving basket.

> Giving is one of the powers that let you kick ass the most in life.

CHAPTER 17:

ACCEPTANCE

EVERY DAY MAY NOT BE GOOD, BUT THERE'S SOMETHING GOOD IN EVERY DAY.
—Unknown

Acceptance is a beautiful state, but we fight it. The transitions in our lives will lead to growth. But acceptance can be challenging. Sometimes, we fight it. Imagine you walk around, see a beautiful red rose, and say, "Go away, I wanted a yellow tulip today!" You deny the beauty of the rose's red, her slender stem, and her delicate being and miss out on one of nature's gifts. You do not appreciate what's in front of you and tell yourself you will not be happy till you see a yellow tulip. Why not be happy with the red rose now and later again when the yellow tulip appears?

Acceptance Is the Beginning of Self-Birth

We grow when we listen to ourselves. Distractions fall away and our voice comes to the surface. We experience self-birth. When you gain acceptance, you stop wasting valuable energy and wanting to fight the present. What is more beautiful than now? Accept it and grow. We deny ourselves this elevated state because we desperately want to control situations we are in. Control is not always helpful. We know deep inside, after years of living on our beautiful planet, that control is often futile. Control just lengthens suffering.

Acceptance Commits You Fully in the Now

Living in the moment is the most beautiful feeling to have. In this state you're not thinking about the future, which often gives anxiety, and not re-experiencing the past, which reminds us of regrets. Experience peace by living fully in the now.

> The most important days of your life are happening now.

There are moments when we are forced to accept the now: a shocking event happens, a death, the loss of a job, a disease, or a confrontation with a dear person. Why wait for these situations to happen and have to accept the present forcefully? Learn to accept daily life now. It gives peace, it gives happiness, it gives power, it gives you, you. After fighting it, it hurts less if you just accept the now. If we want to progress, we have to take life as it is. This does not mean we let a situation go on forever—it just means we transformed fighting things we cannot change into the power of acceptance.

> Change in a more deliberate way.

How Nature Is Doing It

Do you think the grass blade does not accept its being? A lion, roaming around hungry, could stamp on her any minute, but she still lives her little plant life fully. She bends in a heavy storm, she dances when the wind moves her, and she is made anew when raindrops replenish her. We might not have that goddess body yet, we might not be in the director's chair yet, we might not have been healed from old pain a lover brought us, but by fighting acceptance, we suffer more.

Decrease Suffering by Accepting

Acceptance isn't being passive about your life—it's a motivational act of engaging with your life and the world around you. Acceptance means embracing your circumstances and resources in the moment, and, if you don't like certain things, working to change what you can. It's also being grateful and appreciating what you have and what's around you, just like the little grass blade or the red rose.

Be brave and see acceptance as a present that brings growth. Because of acceptance, you can finally take the time off you've denied yourself. Because of acceptance, you can take a moment to watch the bee pollinating the flowers.

> Tell yourself, I will be flexible next time. Just like the blade of grass, I will let the wind transport me to a heightened state. I will therefore decrease my suffering.

I fought acceptance many times in my life. I did not understand its power. At the time, I had an unhealthy relationship with men, food, and family. I reached a point where I came to peace with all three of them. I am not in a perfect state yet and can still be triggered when old pain is awakened, but I can manage it.

How I Gained Acceptance

On my journey to acceptance, first, I used dating apps less. I did not want to meet men who cherry picked for a quick body to sleep with. I dedicate more of my time to meeting men offline. You can meet qualified people and develop an authentic relationship if you venture out. I had had enough of some of the conversations online that started with the lazy two-letter word *hi*.

Second I made peace with food. I saw food as a healer of pain, the invisible shaman who was easy to meet up with. At the nearest supermarket, relief was stacked up on the shelves, from chocolate, to ice cream, to cookies, to cake, to all other sugary stuff that would temporarily kill my pain. I finally accepted food for what it is, food, nothing more, nothing less. I stopped making it into medicine. The days of two pints of Häagen-Dazs to eat my sorrows away are finally gone. You are welcome, Häagen-Dazs, for all the money I made you. I still love you, but my belly does not need you anymore. I am going for the green smoothies now!

Then my family. There is a saying that goes, "Show me a healthy family, and I will show you a dysfunctional one." Many of us have our ups and downs with family. I have now released them from my mind. Why let them occupy precious space and create more anxiety in my life? I see my family now as soothing background music. It is still there, I hear it, but the music is soft and in the background; it is not overwhelming anymore. It is not a loud song that I constantly give attention to, or need to get up to turn off because it gives me a headache. They are there nicely in the background, and I will attend to them when I can.

Acceptance Frees You from Anxiety

Carl Jung said that what you resist will persist.

I resisted those three things, men, food, and family, and the anxiety kept coming back. The wounds were not healed yet, only partially. If you do not accept what your subconscious mind wants, it will keep bugging you till one day you have to listen. That might not come at the most convenient moment in your life, so try to accept things now, before you land in a crisis. One day you will wake up and say, "Holy guacamole, why oh why did I not do that earlier? Why did I not accept my situation before, so I could change faster?" That is thinking in hindsight. It can be helpful but is not beneficial.

Be Grateful You Are Working on It Now

What can you do now? That is the question to focus on.

Be grateful when you find the power to change, the strength to accept current situations and therefore the ability to change. We already know many things in life, but we do not let them sink in deeply enough or take the proper actions on them. Just remember, you are working on it now, and that is the most important thing. Things you need to work on will continue to come to the surface until you learn to accept them, so how can you activate acceptance in your life?

Start with Silence

For me, again, the best recipe to so many ailments in life is good old silence. Practice the power of silence by welcoming it into your life daily. There is this saying I love: "Most problems in the world are created because most people cannot sit in a room by themselves for more than thirty minutes." Think about that. What is it with us human beings, so afraid to know ourselves? Why not find your inner treasures?

Why would you not want to delve into your sanctuary and explore your inner beauty? How do you find your silence? It can be in your room, in a garden, in a park, at work, on a train ride, or in any other place. Going into nature is my favorite place to find silence. You can meditate and observe without judging.

The Future Will Be Better

It is powerful to believe that the future will be better. Accepting now does not mean that it will stay like this forever. Acceptance just means that for now, this present moment, you let pain or inconvenience happen, so it can do its work. Nothing is stagnant. Everything flows and moves in nature, from the river, to the birds, to the clouds. They all change just like you, but at the same time accept the situation now.

Say Thank You to the Pain

I believe pain does not always come into our lives to hurt us; it comes to save us. Pain holds a mirror up to us so we finally see what needs to be done. In my case, it was knee pain. One minute, I felt super, after decades of hating exercise. Then I injured my knee. I wanted to go outside so badly and run and fight my injury. So I told myself there was no pain. I would still run, but I would recalibrate myself. I did not accept that I could not run. Then I realized that was crazy, and I let acceptance take over. I asked myself, what is the gift I am receiving? What is the lesson here? What is this current situation telling me?

I realized that if I kept running I would damage my knees. I would put more strain on them and might not be able to walk for months. I would end up with crutches like those unfortunate winter sport enthusiasts. Is that what I wanted? No! Thank you, acceptance, for showing me the way.

> Thank you, pain, for making me make wiser decisions.

I took it easy for a month. This extra time gave me the best thinking time ever. I was able to take a few steps back and reassess. I realized my knees needed less pressure while running, so I could keep injuries from happening again in the future. I found out how to be a better runner, research I neglected to do before. I thought that running was just an easy thing to learn—it is not!—but there are important techniques to make it easier. Better running methods mean fewer injuries. Through acceptance of my current situation and staying calm, I came out stronger. Understand that when pain comes, it's trying to tell you something. Instead of feeling bad, or mad at the world, use it to dissect what the message is.

> Let patience be your leader and guide you to an answer.

CHAPTER 18:

MORE TIME ALONE

> WE NEED SOLITUDE, BECAUSE WHEN WE'RE ALONE, WE'RE FREE FROM OBLIGATIONS, WE DON'T NEED TO PUT ON A SHOW, AND WE CAN HEAR OUR OWN THOUGHTS.
> —Tamim Ansary

It was a regular morning, or so I thought. I had an exciting new work opportunity where I would learn on the job and at the same time go to school. It was one of those combined work/study situations in the field of technology, which I was exploring.

I was seventeen and had done an aptitude test, and the result was that I had talent for technology. Really? Me? The one who had trouble finding something as simple as a power cord? Oh well, I thought, it is the outcome of a test, so there must be some truth in it, so let me do something with it to help me find my trajectory in life. I had to find a company where I could be an intern, learn the ropes of the trade, and still be able to go to school. It needed to be a company related to the technical classes I took at school. This was not an easy task. At that time women were not working in technical jobs in factories, only men. Especially not at a paper factory I applied at, where four hundred men worked and not one single woman walked around between the giant machines with rolls of paper. But I was persistent. I kept telling them that I wanted to work at their paper factory. This was the right place for me, and they would be happy. Looking back from today's perspective, I now see that the paper factory was a sign that led me later in life to work with paper—writing.

I got an internship, and I was the first woman they'd ever hired in production. I was proud that my persistence paid off. I would work hard to make it a success. But then destiny wanted something else for me.

On a particular uneventful morning I crossed the street to go to work. I saw a car driving up and thought, "I can make it to the other side in time, and if not, he will stop. They always stop, right? Let me hurry, instead of waiting till he drives by. The faster I run, the sooner I will be in the factory." I calculated I could make it in time. I calculated wrong. The driver did not stop, and his car hit my knees.

The man jumped out of his car, completely shocked, and asked if I was okay. I looked at his scared face and was more worried about him than about myself.

"Oh, I am okay. Nothing is wrong with me. I thought I had more time."

I ended up apologizing instead of letting him

express his fault. I did this because I did not want to be late for work. Getting cops out to fill out an accident report and arriving late at work was not something I was looking forward to. Especially since I just started working there and did not want to make a fool out of myself—even though I'd been hit by a car and gotten my knees crushed. I convinced him I was okay. He gave me some money and drove away.

I went to the factory, and I felt the pain intensify. When I told them I was just hit by a car, they sent me home immediately. "Ahhh," I thought, "There goes my plan to become the first female process operator in a paper factory in Limburg," the state I lived in.

But something better happened. I was forced to go home and spend a whole month alone, giving me a lot of time to think about my past, my present, and my future. I had to go to physical therapy and recover from the hit on my knees. That time alone was the first time in my life that my only activity was to lie down, sit up, burp, think, lie down again, eat, and think more. If you have a lot of time alone, first, you go crazy, especially an active person like me. I do not drink coffee, but with my energy, you would think I drink ten cups a day. It was hard not to have an outlet for all my built-up energy. Staying home alone with my thoughts in my newly rented house was hell.

But hell turned out to be kind of a heaven. I developed a vision and an answer to the outcome of my future. I would never have come up with these conclusions if I had not spent this time alone. I realized at this young age how spending time alone is crucial so we can think more deeply, be more focused, and be without the distractions of the outside world.

I decided that I did not belong in the city of Maastricht after all. It is a great city, one of the oldest in the Netherlands, but a city that kept me stuck. I would be a prisoner in my own city, so I decided to move to Amsterdam, the capital of the Netherlands, where life would be free, exciting, and new—the three important ingredients I needed in my life.

When dedicating yourself to time alone, forced or not, you come up with life-changing ideas. I was forced to take this alone time because of my accident, but you can schedule it in without additional strain. Also, not everybody needs a full month. You can come up with life-changing ideas in a few hours. Time alone is healing, revealing, necessary, helpful, and empowering. Why do many of us not schedule this in enough? The first answer that often comes up is lack of time, and this might be true for some of us.

For instance, single parents can have a hard time creating alone time. Many of us are busy with obligations. But it's worth it. Time alone is liberating. Tell yourself that from the Buddha to the emperors who ruled, all of them took time off alone to renew, reenergize, and empower themselves.

Some do not seek alone time because they might feel lonely. If you feel this way, tell yourself this is not real loneliness. This is time to create. This time helps build your future and helps you understand your life.

Acknowledge the importance of quality time alone. What are the advantages you gain by creating this time alone in your life?

1. **You can do more independent thinking.** You will come up with quality thoughts. When you are around friends or family and ask for advice, they will give you advice from their perspective. Learn to develop your own ideas. It is good to receive feedback from friends, but see their advice as the cherry on top. You are the creator of the cake itself.
2. **There is no peer pressure.** When you ask others, they will give you the answers and ideas that are common within a community, a work situation, or a certain culture. The ideas or answers are influenced by past systems they function in. If you create from your inside, alone, then you come up with original thoughts. Less influence from the outside gives you more clarity.
3. **You will be stronger.** You will get to know yourself better, build resilience, grow faster, and evolve differently. You will build mental strength. Imagine yourself in a cocoon growing, changing, and then developing into a butterfly. The cocoon is alone the whole time. It creates its own transformation. Your mental strength will improve, and after a certain amount of time, you will have wings. Let this gestation process develop so you can fly.
4. **You will increase your productivity.** When you find time alone, you will do more than when

you are with others. When you are with your friends you will most likely not take a notebook out and write down the ten steps that will take you from your present situation to a better one. You want to have fun with friends. When you are on the couch watching a movie with your friend, you will probably not write a mission statement for the next thirty years. Productivity comes when you schedule valuable time alone.
5. **You can focus better.** How will your focus be on new ideas when you are with your friend and hear her talk, laugh, or tell stories about the guy who was a jerk on her last date? You can't focus, right? You are committed to the present moment happening in front of you. Focus is a superpower; make sure to make it a priority. Have focused alone time to achieve greatness!
6. **Time alone is better for your creativity.** It sparks eureka moments.

The Best Did It

> The best in history took dedicated time alone frequently.

Not all of us have the privilege to rent a cabin in the woods or a house in the Mediterranean to have this time alone. This is also not necessary. It can be done in our present lives. Be creative in how you schedule in your alone time. It can be done. Create this alone time in your current life situation. Have it first thing in the morning when waking up, by taking a walk to let thoughts percolate, or by unplugging from all electronic devices and going into nature.

How can you create wonderful ideas if you are constantly on social media to see if you've received additional likes? Give these likes to yourself instead by taking a break from the online world and coming up with spectacular thoughts! Numerous studies have found out that people who enjoy alone time experience less depression, have increased levels of happiness, enjoy improved stress management, have better life satisfaction, and reach their goals faster.

CHAPTER 19:

READING BOOKS

YOU WILL BE THE SAME PERSON IN FIVE YEARS AS YOU ARE TODAY EXCEPT FOR THE PEOPLE YOU MEET AND THE BOOKS YOU READ.
—Charlie "Tremendous" Jones

Something exciting in Germany in 1400.

Thank you Johannes Gutenberg for being born in Germany in 1400 and inventing something that became the most important invention of the second millennium. We bow to you with gratitude. You helped bring books and learning to the masses. Your invention was a catalyst in bringing the Renaissance and the Scientific Revolution to humanity. The printing press was created in China, but the invention of the Gutenberg press was a tremendous improvement and helped us move away from only having handwritten manuscripts. What would have happened if you had not bestowed your gift to us? Would we still have impractical large dinosaur-sized books, or would somebody else have invented a printing press? I am grateful it happened when it happened, because billions of people can now read physical books and add wisdom to their lives. What joy books are! They are life changing! They are uplifting and show us the way when we have lost track of everything. What other physical object out there, that costs as little as ten bucks, can bring a lifetime of change?

Some books change you for a day, some books change you for a decade, and some books change the trajectory of your life—they change who you are. What books have you read that caused you to take massive action because the writer inspired you, after reading it, to jump out of your bed and make a gigantic change?

For me, several books have completely altered my life. I started reading at a young age. I loved books, even the books in school. I dove into them. I forgot time. I took lots of notes and was lost in the material, and my imagination roamed around the world with the knowledge I gained.

What Are the Books You've Reread?

The most important books in life are the ones you read again and again. They are sending you an important message about who you are. What books do you reread every year or decade? Make a list of them and see if there is a commonality. They inspire, keep reminding you what to do, and nudge you to go for your dreams. You go back to them for empowerment. They remind you of their wisdom, fun, suspense, or excitement. Books have it all. They are one of the greatest gifts that humans created. Books are powerful and help us live meaningful lives.

Once a Romantic, Always a Romantic

In the beginning I only read fiction. When I was in my teens, I bought cheap romance novels at the local supermarket. I loved romance! Maybe that is why I am still such a hopeless romantic; I read many of those rosy-colored romance novels that cost a buck at the store. Those were the books that stirred up my fantasy first.

Later I changed into more substantial reading. I delved into biographies, philosophy books, poetry, and more nonfiction. I believe a great book is not only there to entertain, but also to help and inspire us *to take action*.

Books Nudge Us to Take Action

The writer's words stimulate one's emotions and intellect and make you think differently. In my twenties, I was a fan of *Oprah* and ordered the self-help books of her guests. I still refer to books from that time of my life—more than twenty-five years ago!

Books changed how I saw the world. One of the first books that changed me exponentially was a little gem by Deepak Chopra, *The Seven Spiritual Laws of Success*. In this book, Deepak takes us on a journey where we learn the seven laws of life, which are practical and help with the fulfillment of dreams. One idea in particular has remained with me, two questions he asked in the last law. In the law of dharma or purpose in life, he wrote, "Ask yourself, if money was no concern and you had all the time and money in the world, what would you do? If you would still do what you currently do, then you are in dharma, because you have *passion* for what you do—you are expressing your unique talents. Then ask yourself: How am I best suited to serve humanity? Answer that question and put it into practice."

This was life changing for me. It transformed me from living my life without meaning to living with meaning. At that time I was in my twenties, when I worked at the bank. Working there was not my passion. Instead, I worked to earn money, make my bosses happy, and "survive" this thing called life.

Some Books Change You for Life

Deepak Chopra's question unplugged me from my boring job and set me up for a life where I joined the arts. The arts are where I feel at home and useful because I get to help people with the things I create. My books, my quotes, my poems come from a deep passionate place within my heart. They are created with love. I am grateful that I found Deepak's book at the right time in my life. Not long after I read his book I went to hear him speak at a lecture in the Netherlands. I still remember that evening. I remember what dress I had on. I remember how I felt. I remember what I said too. I told him that his book changed my life. I looked into his dark eyes and saw a depth of knowledge. I'm grateful he shared his wisdom in this little gem. Read it this short and to-the-point book, and you, too, will find answers on how to find passion and live it.

A Novel in a Year

Louise Doughty's book, *A Novel in a Year*, gave me that gentle push that I desperately needed. Her practical and abounding book encouraged me to finally finish my novel. Louise said it could be done in one year, and I believed her! I acted on her advice.

I got introduced to her book in 2009. I used to volunteer at NPR, and one of the perks was receiving free books from publishing houses that hoped journalists at NPR would write about them. I gathered stacks of books every week, and luckily, *A Novel in a Year* was one of them.

I made a start with reading in 2009, but it wasn't till December 2017 that I committed to reading the book more deliberately and let its advice sink in. Her golden advice was, "Put on your shoes. You are going to visit your novel." It was the golden advice I needed. I had to go to Spain, where my character from another book I was working on would be from, and experience the culture, food, monuments, and architecture firsthand. Through my words, I would create him, bring him to life, show him loving people, and hear his beating heart. Louise's book gave me the confidence to look for him, so I booked a flight to Spain a few days later. My character Happio is now alive, found his bliss, and is happy. I gave him a life, and he is now out there helping others.

I love when a book is practical, contains useful information I can apply to my life, *and* is well written. I also enjoy when the writer's love for the subject shines true. Write your own novel in a year if that is one of your dreams!

Another thing Louise said in the book is, "You can make money doing this." That line imprinted in my mind did its magic. Yes, I could be an author, bring value and meaning to my readers, and at the same time turn it into my profession and earn money while doing it.

Many other books changed me as well, and I will write down a few for you to read at the end of this chapter, but for now let's continue on other notes about reading books.

Just One Principle Is Enough

Ralph Waldo Emerson said it best, "I cannot remember the books I've read any more than the meals I have eaten; even so, they have made me."

It's okay if you don't retain everything. The important thing is immersing yourself in a topic or story; it's life changing. After a week of reading, I sometimes think, "What the heck was written in that book again?" Commit to remembering just one principle from a book that stands out.

> Just one principle is all you need to take from a book and is good enough to start with.

Visit Book Stores!

There is nothing as fun and exciting as roaming in a bookstore and finding that book that has been waiting to find you. It happens if you are open to it! Go to regular bookstores, but also visit second-hand bookstores. I love the smell: old paper and history! I often ask for recommendations from the staff that work there. You could ask them something like, "What are the books you reread?" The answer is often surprising, and I've received great tips that way. One of the best tips came from a bookstore staffer who recommended *Letters to a Young Poet*, by Rilke. I was already familiar with that little book but had never read it. It is a gem of a book that is timeless, fast to read, and will make you feel great.

Rainer Maria Rilke

This phenomenal writer gave me approval to be an artist with the help of his writings. He showed me the way where there was a vague path before. He cleared up the mist in the woods and guided me to an open field, where I found my creativity. He conveyed that when I said a full yes to being an artist and following my creativity, I would succeed in life. This helped me grow when I was finding my way during my existential crisis.

Everything else had to comply with me being an artist. I had to set my life up around my writings. I had to find work that supported me in continuing to write, jobs that gave me the flexibility, time, and money, so I could have weeks of uninterrupted writing time. He told me to use my unique voice, a voice created from my depth, from my deepest sanctuary, instead of copying others. He taught me to first understand my art before I gave birth to it. He reminded me how important patience is, that patience is everything and everything revolves around it. He taught me not to rush and be "too early" and immature with my art output.

Rilke expressed that solitude was a beautiful thing where artists found all they needed. Solitude was not to be ashamed of and needed to be searched for since it creates exciting art with depth.

> Rilke opened my heart wide open and poured his love in to feed me. I could go unapologetically after my wildest dreams and become an author.

The Marshmallow Experiment!

One of the things I keep reading about in self-help books is the *marshmallow experiment*. If I read about these marshmallows one more time, I will honestly go crazy. Can there be a cake experiment? Or a pie experiment, maybe? Not the same fucking and annoying marshmallows again! I am still, after many years of reading over and over about this experiment in books, not sure if I was the kid who would have waited or not. In my present state, I will wait. Find this experiment online if you have not read about it yet. Decide to read more books so they will give you superpowers.

Where Do You Read?

Will you read at home, in nature, or inside a coffee shop? Usually I read deep books at home, and I often read inspiring books in nature. Being out in nature is already an inspiring thing. When you read a book outdoors, you will receive double the power. In coffee shops I usually read nonfiction. The surrounding talks, walks, or coughs often disturb me, and a nonfiction book lends itself better to pausing more often. When I am in a magical fiction story and my imagination needs to roam undisturbed, a busy environment is not always beneficial. Through constant reading you get thousands of perspectives from exciting minds and develop a richer life in the process.

The place where you read can empower you because its magic will reinforce what you read. I once read in front of the Arch of Hadrian, in Athens, Greece. Everything I read was instilled by the power of this Roman emperor. I felt him around me while I was reading. He was a brilliant leader and built projects that endure his legacy. He established cities, and the Arch of Hadrian was constructed by the citizens of Athens as an honor for him founding their city. Find mind-blowing, inspiring places, and read there to stimulate your mind with the greatness around.

Reading can take you to faraway places. Through constant reading you experience thousands of perspectives from exciting minds and develop a richer life in the process. Here are books I love and that have changed my life:

The Seven Spiritual Laws of Success by Deepak Chopra
The Alchemist by Paulo Coelho
The First and Last Freedom by Krishnamurti
Tao Te Ching by Lao Tzu
Siddhartha by Herman Hesse
A Novel in a Year by Louise Doughty
Flow by Mihaly Csikszentmihalyi
Mindset by Carol S. Dweck
Think and Grow Rich by Napoleon Hill
Poems by Rumi
Metamorphosis by Franz Kafka
Arabian Nights and Days by Naguib Mahfouz
Meditations by Marcus Aurelius
A Moveable Feast by Ernest Hemingway
Man's Search for Meaning by Victor Frankl
Recollections: An Autobiography by Victor Frankl

The Little Prince by Antoine de Saint-Exupéry
Selected Writings by Ralph Waldo Emerson
Wild by Cheryl Strayed
Sapiens by Yuval Noah Harari
Thinking Fast and Slow by Daniel Kahneman
This Is Water by David Foster Wallace

Happy Reading!

CHAPTER 20:

CREATING COMMUNITIES

IF YOU WANT TO GO FAST, GO ALONE. IF YOU WANT TO GO FAR, GO TOGETHER.
—African Proverb

Start creating communities to feel empowered. You can organize them yourself or join groups you are interested in. Showing up is key!

When I visit cafés, I see people not talking to each other. Most have music on, are focused on their computer or phone, and have little face-to-face connection. People aren't connecting the way they did in the past.

> Connecting with people you don't know is fun because they have the potential to become new friends.

Loneliness in society worries me. Many people do not have communal support. Social media has made us detached, and it's often a poor substitute for personal interaction. More time on devices means less interaction with people, which causes loneliness. People do not talk effortlessly to each other like other generations did. Though it can be a place to find people with your interests, social media is often a cheap substitute for a real community.

We Have to Change This, People!
Bring back spontaneous interactions. They enrich our lives. I am impressed when someone I just met starts a conversation in a restaurant, a coffee shop, or any other public place. It is healthy to begin a relationship this way. Being online works for some, but when you meet in real life, it adds magic to the encounter. Energy sparks fly in the air, which you do not experience online.

Put Devices Away at Times
Our devices take time away from real-life connections. That is why certain places have started a trend promoting laptop-free hours. I have seen it in Paris and lately also in Los Angeles. I dare you to leave your devices at home. Initially, it will be hard. You might feel that you've left your arm or leg at home. But it is empowering to hide *less* behind our screens. The first step is to acknowledge codependence.

Get Out There!
Nothing is as powerful as looking people in their eyes, catching their smile, and seeing their tilted

face because you interacted with them. You will experience life anew when you go out and explore your environment and new places, tasting the fresh air, meeting interesting people, connecting with others in real life, and feeling their energy around. We light up in the presence of other people. They bring us joy. Plan on having outings every week. You can visit book signings, meetups, museums, parks, movie screenings, libraries, or the local coffee shop. Get out there and connect with others. I am planning to visit more book signings this year. They are often free, and many curious and interesting people visit them.

Find Your Niche
If you want to increase your sociability and play a more powerful role in your community, then you can become an organizer for events. You will create a space for others and can cultivate an interesting group of people and make connections with like-minded individuals.

I wanted to decrease loneliness around me and decided something needed to be done. It would help me and at the same time, others as well. I, too, had been alone at home and often felt disconnected.

Gandhi said, "If we could change ourselves, the tendencies in the world would also change. As a man changes his own nature, so does the attitude of the world change toward him . . . We need not wait to see what others do."

I wanted to *be the change* that I wanted to see in the world, like Gandhi hinted upon in his quote. I thought starting communities would help us all. I wanted to produce fun events where people could gather, learn new things, meet cool people, eat yummy food, and in the end become less lonely. Being alone is helpful when you're giving yourself the time you need and connecting with yourself, but being in this state for too long will disconnect you from the social energy we all need. We grow when we make connections. Magic happens, and joy is created. Becoming an organizer was one of the best things I ever did. Not only did I make friends through my groups, but I also helped others with their progress.

Find something that interests you. The first group I created was about ideas. I adore them and see them like ships appearing on the horizon and getting closer. It is important when the ship arrives at the dock that you get on board. A quote I love is, "Twenty years from now you will be more disappointed by the things that you didn't do than by the ones you did do. So, throw off the bowlines. Sail away from the safe harbor. Catch the trade winds in your sails. Explore. Dream. Discover." Ideas are like seeds—they begin small but end up growing into something beautiful and divine.

Find Your Group

The first group I organized was The Idea Meetup for Curious People.

Curiosity is a prerequisite for coming up with ideas. I wanted a group of open-minded people to mingle so I could see their curiosity flow with others. I also wanted to meet curious people—I am inspired by individuals who love ideas.

Here's how I did it: I was on Meetup and transitioned into an organizer. It is not difficult. You pay an organizer fee, upload pictures, and describe your group. But what is not hard is not necessarily easy. You have to find a way to make your group pop and stand out from other groups. A gazillion groups start every day. Make sure yours is unique. Think quality first. People will take time off and fight traffic to drive to your event. Make it memorable—under promise and over deliver.

Next, find a space for your event. Especially in the beginning as a new organizer, be nimble and stay resourceful. My first event was at the Pickwick Café in West Hollywood. I asked Melissa, a friend if she knew of a space. Especially when low on financial resources, work with what you have. Do not be afraid to ask around. Also ask your group members.

Value for Everybody

I brought people into the venue, and they would pay for drinks and food. It was a win-win situation for all, though it could have been more successful. I learned valuable lessons at that gathering. One is that you have to make the group *specific*. I announced a group for curious people with ideas but did not specify the topic. It was not targeted enough, and I had not made an agenda. That's the second thing I learned: Always have an agenda. It can be a simple one. Because there was no agenda, some attendees ended up telling lengthy personal stories. The focus was not on ideas. That brings me to the third lesson: As the group organizer, always bring it back to the topic and be super clear about time limits.

My Second Group

Learning from my first group, I brainstormed and thought deeply about the future of humanity, but first looked into the present to find a topic to discuss. The biggest thing out there, without a doubt, was the Internet. I asked myself, What will be bigger than the Internet in the coming years? What would take over the Internet? My answer was the *Internet of things*. This is a scenario where everything is connected through sensors that live their lives without interaction from humans. Sensors provide data and connect with each other. The Internet as we know it would eventually go away, and we would live in this *Internet of things*. Humans can make errors operating machines; often a machine can do it better without fault. Let's say a machine operator is tired, working two shifts, and did not react fast enough to a calamity. A computer does not get tired and can be programmed to do several actions at the same time. I thought that was an interesting topic to explore. There was a lot of power in the *Internet of things*.

Naiveté Brings You Far

I did not know anything about the *Internet of things*. Nothing at all, zero. It was a field that computer programmers, futurists, high-level tech people, and other smart and progressive people delved into, but me, a banker turned actress, knew nothing about this. But looking back, it turned out to be a great thing. Naiveté can take you far. Be honest and say that you are passionate about learning about the field but are still a novice. Experts in a field appreciate that because they are often long-time learners. I started my group because I wanted to fast-track my learning.

I started IoT LA. I researched the topic and then connected with the thought leaders in this field. At that time there was no IoT community in Los Angeles. At the first meetup, seventeen people showed up, and I brought my homemade food, wines, snacks, and freshly baked little chocolate cakes. It was held at one of the top tech companies in LA. I was fortunate to get this place, because I knew then that it would be a big success. One of the members who had signed up for my group offered me the place. It was a fun gathering, and we all enthusiastically committed to coming to the next event. I just had to organize the next one, and I did. It made me feel good because I brought strangers together and created a platform for them to connect.

You Will Get Help—Just Start!

Create communities and feel empowered by providing safe and fun places. People are grateful for others who take initiative and start a group they are interested in.

Come up with a good format, and then put your group online and make sure to add appealing pictures, great copy, and a reason why they should sign up for your group. Then, schedule your first event. You will learn a lot about the interactions of the attendees and what you can improve. When your group starts growing, instead of paying for everything, find sponsorships. I told companies that I would love to visit and bring smart members. Often I asked if they had a speaker, too, that could talk about what their company did. They loved that because they could now become a member of the community without organizing it. I did all the work, but they provided food, drinks, the place, and the speaker. So build your group up one person at a time. Remember quality always wins. That will keep people coming back. Treat your group like your child, with care and awe.

Start a knitting group. Start a book club. Start a sport buddies group. It does not matter what you start; it matters that you tried something new. You super organizer, go! My tech groups had more than two thousand members when I closed them down. It was successful, and several people told me it was their favorite tech group to go to. It was also free—after a few events, I was able to secure valuable sponsorships. And the best part was the valuable friendships I made.

You never know what will come out of starting something yourself.

Start with the Top

If you want to start a group and you're looking for sponsorships or a company to host you, reach for the top. Find the decision-makers. It's easier if you can talk to the owner first.

Most of my events happened because of this strategy. Go to places where the founders speak. Tell them that you have a group of interesting people and would love to introduce them to their company. If you cannot reach them, then write a super letter. Put yourself in the shoes of the reader. Why do you want to bring your group there? How will it help them? What can you help them with besides just showing up and eating all their food? Why should their limited marketing budget go to *your* group?

My group had lots of smart people, so that was my unique selling point. I told them it was a prime opportunity for everyone to network. What happened organically is that people got job offers because they mingled with the company's workers. Always invite people who work at the sponsoring company too! At one event, during the mixer, some attendees were offered jobs on the spot. I did not find out until later, but a software engineer at another event told me, "By the way, I got hired at your last event." Nice! I love that I could help people find work.

The Reward as An Organizer

As the community organizer, you will learn a lot, from public speaking, to getting sponsorships, to making valuable connections for everybody involved. It will help you grow as a person. By the way, people will appreciate you, and you will get things done that were previously inconceivable. For example, you might get to go to conferences that cost thousands of dollars, but you get in for free as an organizer. I held more than thirty successful events in Los Angeles and Orange County. But what made me happiest is that I helped people make connections and as a result, there was less loneliness around. Kick ass as an organizer and bring people together. Let me know what communities you've created or attended.

CHAPTER 21:

SEX TRANSMUTATION OR LESS SEX

SEX IS ALWAYS ABOUT EMOTIONS. GOOD SEX IS ABOUT FREE EMOTIONS; BAD SEX IS ABOUT BLOCKED EMOTIONS.
—Deepak Chopra

I start this chapter with a smile. Who wants less sex? Most of us want more! What are you trying to tell us? Sex is still taboo, but making a case for wanting less sex or a different kind of sex is even more of taboo.

This chapter focuses on how powerful sexual energies can be redirected and transmuted from the physical to the spiritual, making sex a superpower in our lives.

Transfer One Form of Energy into a Different Kind

We do not talk about sex enough, and when we do talk about it, we all are having sex constantly, right? We are Energizer Bunnies, getting our action on. Nonstop. Not!

We as humans are some of the few animals that actually have sex for pleasure, plus there are several benefits of sex, both mentally and physically, so there is no wonder we place such an emphasis on it. But the truth is, there are times when less sex is desirable.

I thought needing less sex was strange, until I read chapter eleven, the tenth step to riches, in Napoleon Hill's self-help classic book *Think and Grow Rich*: "The Mystery of Sex Transmutation."

What I read I had not read in any other book, or let me rephrase, I had not read in popular media. Maybe the material was out there, but I was not lucky enough to have come across it. Popular media advocates physical sex, since it sells.

Big dollars are generated by promoting this super emotion. Napoleon Hill wrote that people seldom become successful before they turn forty. Once in their forties, the successful ones stopped chasing the physical expression of the emotion of sex. Sexual energy gets transformed into something more powerful, to a more spiritual force, I learned.

"Sex transmutation is simple and easily explained. It means the switching of the mind from thoughts of physical expressions to thoughts of some other nature."

Most people after forty stop overindulging in the physical expression of sex. At this point, sex has other possibilities. There are other ways to use this strong and complicated emotion. Powerful stuff, I thought. When I read it for the first time, I had not yet experienced a lower sex drive, but later on, I had no sex at all for two years. I decided to give this sex transmutation thing a chance. I found myself partnerless and wanted to see how it would change me. I wanted to transmute my power from the physical to the spiritual. I did not date for those two years. I had sexual feelings but let them come out differently.

I let my sexual energy fuel my creativity instead of acting on it. I postponed intimacy, because when you have not done it for a while, you become pickier. You will find yourself thinking, "No, this is not the one who will get me out of celibacy," "I've waited a while now. I can wait a bit longer," and "I do not want that guy in my bed." Looking back on those two "sexless" years, I have to say that those were two of the most productive years in my life. If you are at home now and thinking or feeling bad about not having enough sex in your life, then try this sex-transmutation thing Napoleon Hill advocated.

> Replace feelings like feeling sorry for yourself, at home alone, as a "sexless" human, into empowering feelings that you can feel sexy but in different ways.

For some of us who have not experienced sexuality for a while, do not despair. You just have to learn to change this powerful sexual force you have inside of you into something even more powerful. Hill was onto something. In those two sexless years, I started my hot sauce company, a clothing company, and several meetup groups. I did all the things I'd postponed before, with a targeted focus. I still felt my sexuality, but was not looking for a physical outlet for it. Because of my temporary pause on dating, I became successful in non-relationship-related areas, like my business endeavors. I once read that Leonardo da Vinci did not date much. I am not saying to stop dating to become successful, but sometimes a little break can be life changing. I liked this strategy so much that years later I did this again. In two years of not having any sex I ran three marathons and wrote three books. I kicked ass, not literally but figuratively. Give it a try. You might become a super productive badass.

Work on Yourself First

We should stay open to meeting others and connecting and seeing if we can be in healthy, joyful relationships, but do this when you're ready. It does not always have to turn into something physical. I am talking especially about compulsive daters: four, five, ten dates a week, every single week. I once went out with a heart surgeon resident, and he told me that he went out on more than two thousand dates in less than two years. I was flabbergasted. TWO THOUSAND? Holy guacamole! How did he do that? He went for a coffee in the morning, an afternoon date, one around 4:00 p.m. once in a while, and often one in the late evenings. He said he learned a lot about women. Wow! I bet he did! I did the calculation: 365 days in a year, four dates in a day, in two years would leave room for 2,920 potential dates if you went at it nonstop every day. What he was saying could be done. But was it desirable? For him it was. What was I doing with my one date a week in previous years? Just kidding here; I am okay with it. I could have never mustered time for two thousand dates. He was a resident too; weren't they supposed to have no free time at all while being in those brutal residency years? Or was he a superhuman already? He definitely kicked some ass—wink, wink.

There is power in saying no to our sexual drives and using that energy for something else. Have you stayed with a guy or a girl overnight and thought, "I should not have done that?" Sex depletes powerful energy, and when it's used up with somebody we do not want to be with, it's life energy that's lost. I became super picky about whom I slept with later on. I would rather read a good book than go on a date where I felt the guy chose me like an Amazon product that popped up on his screen.

I wanted to dedicate more time to myself, my businesses, my thoughts, and my new strategies. I gave myself time to work on me. A better me would become a more desirable partner later on. When I reached some of my goals and became a better person in the process, I would be open again to a potential partner.

I transformed sexual energy into drive, motivation, and energy of a higher order. The concept of sex transmutation says that when you use sex extensively, leaked energy goes out through your sexual organs. Instead, let that energy go through your mind. When you see the results of doing this for months, you will be in awe. It has been popular for years in Eastern philosophy, but we are just scratching the surface of it in the West. This is mind-blowing truth compared to all the sex advertising we get bombarded with every day. Sure, sex sells, but it can hold us back if we use it in the wrong way. Why not hold your horses, figuratively speaking, and not always go for it? Use it in other ways, ways that will transform your life.

How Can You Approach This Sex Transmutation Thing?

When you feel sexual energy forming in your body, let it lead you to create a masterpiece instead. Let it inspire you to write a beautiful poem, paint an exquisite painting, write a beautiful piece of prose, or anything else that brings out your creativity. Now go read that chapter in Napoleon Hill's book. It helped me harness my sexual energies and transform them into powerful and creative creations. If you are in a relationship and you are happy, do not do what I advise in this chapter, unless your partner agrees to participate as well. I do not want anyone to be deprived of anything, if you know what I mean—wink, wink. I just did this sex transmutation experiment because I was single. My creativity has flourished! Now excuse me while I go find that cute Italian boy—ha-ha, just kidding!

CHAPTER 22:

DISCIPLINE

DISCIPLINE IS THE BRIDGE BETWEEN GOALS AND ACCOMPLISHMENT.
—Jim Rohn

A tree is standing tall and strong in the meadow. The sun shines on her leaves, illuminating her all around. Her beauty is majestic. Her roots keep her grounded.

Discipline is the strong root that you need to live your best life. The more discipline you can instill in yourself, the more grounded you will be and the better able to succeed. Discipline is not for the faint of heart. Many see discipline as something that takes the fun away, something to ignore so we can overeat, overdrink, or do other things to avoid the obvious problems in front of us. Let me make a case here that if you don't learn to love discipline, you will not create a life you will love. Basta!

....
Discipline brings everything that you love into your life.
....

Discipline helps us to finish things; discipline makes the impossible a reality. Discipline changes worthless lives into meaningful powerhouses. Learn from discipline like the most devoted student. It is the master enabler. Discipline is like the blood and heartbeat that keep your body thriving.

Nike said it wisely, "Just do it."

Start, Continue, and Finish

This is what it often comes down to. Discipline helps you to keep going because nothing gets done without discipline. Live your life with discipline as your new best friend. What can you do if you aren't feeling disciplined?

Forgive Yourself

Nobody is perfect. If you are having a hard time today, so be it. Maybe you had a super-busy schedule this week. Maybe you did not sleep well. Do not beat yourself up; instead, be kind, forgive yourself, and then proceed with your tasks. There is always a tomorrow or a later in the afternoon. Kick negativity out so you can take action. Forgiveness helps you rise above it all. After forgiveness, you can move on and create your magic.

Connect with Your *Why*

The philosopher Frederick Nietzsche once said, "He who has a why can endure any how." Understanding your why will help you achieve your goals.

Take the time to understand your why, or your purpose. Even if it takes you years to perfectly formulate it, the right why will show you how to win your battle. Living with your why helps you achieve discipline, because you aren't distracted by things that don't help you. You drop all the bullshit like it is nothing.

If you take a moment to think about your why every day, that is, your purpose in life, then you will live a disciplined life.

Get Support from Others
Many people find discipline challenging. Reach out to your friends to get help. I meet up with friends, and we talk about life. Do not feel ashamed or weak asking for help. Others often see the good in us and express what they admire about us, which gives us the power and drive to keep going. Listen to their encouragement and believe them. They know how fantastic you are and how you are kicking ass.

Start Small
This is super important. You cannot go to the gym and pick up the biggest barbell on your first day. You'll feel overwhelmed and won't continue. Take little steps and gradually increase them; over time, you will complete your goal. Appreciate that you have become more disciplined.

Do It for Others

What motivates me often is helping other people. When I fundraised for Haiti, I had hungry people in mind, and that gave me the discipline to keep going for days to make the event happen. Who will you help if you get your shit together and just finish what needs to be done? What friend can you spoil or maybe take on a trip somewhere if you work hard? Feel the power of wanting to help others instill more discipline in you.

> Imagine how you will change people's lives when you finally go for it.

Feel Your Mortality

Life is short, and time is of the essence. When in your teens or twenties, you might not have thought about the end of your life yet, but eventually it is coming to all of us. We all have this in common: one day we die, so get to work. Start now and get it done. You do not want to wait till you are lying in your casket. Kick ass now!

Exercise and Feel Better

If you're not feeling motivated, go for a gratitude walk. Get out and appreciate the fresh air. Walk to the park or even to the supermarket to get a healthy snack. Let exercise put you in a better mood so you can get back on track. Exercise releases built-up frustrations. Better this than eating two pints of ice cream.

Scream It from the Rooftops

Make a public commitment so others will remind you of your goal. There will always be that annoying "Facebook friend" whom you never met in real life that will keep asking, "How are you doing on those ambitious goals of yours?"

Make It Easy to Do

When I started running, I had everything ready for the next day. My shoes and socks were in front of the door, and I only had to step into them. I ran a few minutes in the beginning so I wouldn't be too sore the next day or hate doing it. Make it easy so you can actually continue doing it.

....

Now kick procrastination to the curb and be unstoppable!

....

PART 4:
LIVE AN INTENTIONAL LIFE

CHAPTER 23:
FRIENDSHIPS

> TRUE FRIENDSHIP MULTIPLIES THE GOOD IN LIFE AND DIVIDES ITS EVILS. STRIVE TO HAVE FRIENDS, FOR LIFE WITHOUT FRIENDS IS LIKE LIFE ON A DESERT ISLAND... TO FIND ONE REAL FRIEND IN A LIFETIME IS GOOD FORTUNE; TO KEEP HIM IS A BLESSING.
> —Baltasar Gracián

My favorite description of the start of a friendship is in a little novella, *The Little Prince*, by Antoine de Saint-Exupéry, who was a French aristocrat, writer, poet, and pioneering aviator. He was a true renaissance man, who wrote this little gem in 1943. The book is masterfully written, but I especially cherish the quote that explains the beginning of friendship. The little prince meets the fox and asks him to come and play with him.

The fox answers that he cannot, because he is not tamed yet. "It is something that's been too often neglected. It means 'to create ties.'"

Give Friendships Time to Develop

Be patient with your friends. Let things grow the way they need to grow. Take friendship slow and easy, and respect the boundaries of others. Being a good friend is about understanding your friend's needs. In *The Little Prince*, the notes that explain the beginnings of friendship are a beautiful testimony.

Good Friends Are Like Oxygen

We cannot live without them. What is better than caring, sweet, valuable, honest, fun, critical, giving, loving friends we can count on? There is nothing I cherish more than the good friends I have, who empower me, surprise me, listen to me, spend time with me, caress my heart, heal my wounds, support me in my endeavors, do not judge me, and keep believing in me when others say, "Is it not time to finally get that regular job instead of still believing in that crazy, big dream of yours?"

A Friend Understands the Songs in Our Heart

A friend understands when to be quiet and when to give you an ear. A friend will call you out on your bullshit. Friends are not afraid to tell you what you just did, or what you should not have done. Friends support us in our dream building. A life without good friends is a painful life. We are social beings and need others around us. They inspire and lift us. Whatever you do in life, make sure you surround yourself with good people who believe in you. Some friendships are a space rocket from the beginning. Thank you, Esther and Helene, my besties since I was eighteen, and Jennifer and Chris since my thirties.

In Good and Bad Times

If there is one superpower besides really, really, really, really believing in yourself, it is to keep the right people around you. This is an important decision: Whom do you let into your brain? Whom do you spend valuable time with? Lost time can never come back. Choose your close friends wisely. They become your place to run to and the place to heal your broken heart. You want people who will be there for you in bad times too.

Friends Help Even if It's Not Beneficial for Them

Sometimes doing something for you is inconvenient for your friends, but guess what? They still do it! They are your buddies, your rocks, and your lighthouse. They do it out of the goodness of their heart and because they love you. It hurts me when I lose a friend. Friendship is always a two-way street. Spinoza said that no matter how many times you try to slice a cake, there will always be two sides. Life changes, we change, and friends change, so sometimes we part ways but still wish each other the best. Never forget how your friends helped you.

Be Reliable and Keep Your Promises

Friends are our lighthouses; they show us the way out of the dark. Always be reliable and keep your promises to your friends. And if you cannot do so because of hurt feelings, be honest about it. Nothing is as hurtful as to find out later that a friend lied to you. A newer friend of mine wrote an article saying that you couldn't make old friends again. I thought that was a poignant line. True, you can't, because these friendships took lengthy years to develop, or sometimes decades to nourish.

However, you can make valuable friendships later in life. How do we make new friends? Especially in a cosmopolitan city, it can be challenging sometimes.

Be Proactive

When I moved to Los Angeles, the behavior of Angelinos confused me. I met people who told me their whole life story the first time we met, but then I did not hear from them again. I was confused. Back home, people who expressed intimate details were mostly friends or wanted to be close. I was surprised on several occasions that I did not hear back from the people I had intimate conversations with. You told me your whole fucking life story and the juicy details that came with it, and then disappear?

Then a guy I knew told me, "You reach out first. Do not wait to be disappointed."

Reach Out to Them First

I thought: "Yes, I should. Just waiting till friendships magically happen will probably leave me by myself for years to come." Every time I met a person I thought was special, made me laugh, made me see things differently, was sweet, made my heart smile, I would write, call, text, or communicate with them and tell them that I had a great time and would love to meet up again. I was surprised by how many times people were happy to hear from me! So be the first one. Do not wait for them. Be proactive and be a leader in this. Reach out to the ones you think will enrich your life, and then you enrich their lives in return. Meet a few times and see if it develops into a friendship or you stay acquaintances, which is not bad either.

Be Their Biggest Supporter!

Support your friends when they start a project, reach a precious goal, change jobs, move to another house, or any other event that is emotional or life changing. I remember when I did my Kickstarter for my hot sauce company. I was happy when my friends helped me reach my goal. They could invest as little as ten bucks, so it was not a big financial commitment, but I will always remember those who supported me. I will also remember the ones who did not. The friends who supported me warmed my heart, and it meant so much to me. Be there to support the important projects your friends undertake. They will remember this their entire life. You were there when it mattered most! Stand on the first row and cheer them on! If you do not have the resources now, then write them a little note and say, I would love to support you, but I just cannot do it now. This will let your friend know that you care.

Surprise Them! Surprises Are Fun

Another way to strengthen friendships is to *Surprise* them with a capital S once in a while. Do something they do not expect. Who does not want more surprises in their lives, especially when they come from a good friend? And it is fun for both of you. You can take them to an exciting restaurant or a trip to Europe or write a poem for them. Be generous with your surprises, and you will get many coming your way. Originality is always appreciated.

The Jealous Beast Needs to Go!

Perhaps you and your friend have done similar things—gone to the same classes or met the same people—but one of you is more successful than the other. One is still living paycheck to paycheck, and the other just made her first million. When this happens, jealousy will rear its ugly head. Do not let this ugly head get too big.

Nothing is worth losing decades of friendship over because of another person's success. Do not let jealousy ruin friendships. Be happy for your friends. They worked hard to fulfill their dreams, and if you can be happy for them, they will share their fortune with you. Keep supporting your friends, and do not let jealousy cloud your judgment. This is a big one! Be the best cheerleader, and enjoy the journey together.

Do Not Flash Your Gained Fortunes

The successful friend should stay humble and keep giving her friends love. Do not go missing in action. Do not give a reason to create jealousy. The jealous beast needs to stay away on both sides of the friendship! Although you might have gotten busier due to your success, keep investing in the people who were there before you hit it big. Express to them that you might have been a bit occupied lately, but the love you have for them is still the same. You still value the friendship. Your absence is temporary, building for a better future, but when you get through this hectic phase, you both will be able to celebrate on the roof terrace drinking that delicious champagne. Those glasses will taste so much sweeter because you gave each other the space to go for your dreams instead of letting jealousy come between you.

CHAPTER 24:

GRATITUDE

BE GRATEFUL FOR WHAT YOU ALREADY HAVE WHILE YOU PURSUE YOUR GOALS. IF YOU AREN'T GRATEFUL FOR WHAT YOU ALREADY HAVE, WHAT MAKES YOU THINK YOU WOULD BE HAPPY WITH MORE?
—Roy T. Bennett

Gratitude has saved my little ass literally and figuratively many times. Just this morning, for starters. I stopped at the gas station on my way to a coffee shop to write. My self-imposed deadline for my book was in four days. I filled my empty tank up and fell down with satisfaction in my car seat, with more force than usual.

I heard crackkkkkkkk in slow motion. My pants split open from my waist to the lower part of my butt, to the beginning of my thighs. My butt was totally visible due to the large vertical split. Wow! My favorite fuchsia pants from Italy that I bought on sale were now split in half. My body had received too much nourishment lately, and with a drastic gesture showed me that I should stop consuming so much. My poor fuchsia pants could not handle it anymore and broke down in the parking lot of a busy gas station. Luckily, I was in the car when it happened, and finished with fueling. I drove to a side street, got out, and made sure nobody saw my snow-white behind.

Ahhhh! I was going to be delayed. If I went back home it would take an hour away from my already tight schedule, and neighbors might see my white butt. A few of my neighbors are seventy and older, and I do not want to cause any heart attacks. I remembered a little bag of clothes in the trunk of my car. This bag had been there for ages. It had a white winter coat I bought in freezing Prague, a torn silk top from an Indian store I had planned on fixing for ages, and a skirt I was not sure about keeping or throwing away. I pulled this life-saving skirt out and thanked it with my whole being for still being there. You saved my ass, you little skirt. I will keep you! Why was I wondering for years if I should keep you or not? You saved me from walking around town with an exposed white butt.

Gratitude Comes in Many Forms
Gratitude appears in many different forms, and the more we feel it and fill ourselves up with it, the more it will empower us. Gratitude is a cleanser. It provides us with a blank state. We can be just like a baby looking into the world, not knowing our past or future, just enjoying the present moment. When you practice gratitude often, you enjoy life more. The baby looks around with curious eyes and observes

everything anew. It does not drag itself into the past, does not think about annoying barking dogs, or about unpaid bills, or the need to schedule a dentist appointment. The baby lives in the present and takes it all in. Maybe it burps a bit here and there. The baby is innocent and therefore has no worries, takes life as it is, and embodies love.

Learn from Others Who Practice Gratitude

We should learn from babies and little children and become more present. Gratitude will help you do that. You will see the beauty in the mundane. You will see the mystery in everything—even the hassle of torn fuchsia pants that shows your behind. Ultimately, if we're living with gratitude, everything is okay.

You will get rid of dissatisfaction when instilled with gratitude. You see everything as a present given to you. You do not negotiate with your present or want to change it. You take it all in, breathe deeply, and let things go. You pull yourself out of a state of complacency. It juices your life up.

Gratitude for Oatmeal

While I am writing this chapter in a cute little coffee shop called Trinity, in Echo Park, eating a bowl of oatmeal, I reflect on gratitude. For this present moment, I am extremely grateful for my warm oatmeal in a white porcelain bowl topped with warm oat milk and sprinkled with persimmons and almond slices. I savor every little bite with the most delight. I am grateful that food is plentiful and I have the time to enjoy it.

I am grateful for the oats themselves. The life of an oat was not an easy one. Oats grow from seeds. They are planted in the later part of the year, around autumn. Once in the ground they have a few weeks to germinate before the weather turns colder. Then they wait till the sun shines in spring to grow. When the plant is grown, the farmer harvests the oats.

I am grateful for the people who work day in and day out to make our lives easier. Farmers are definitely part of this category. Thank you, farmers. I never would have this delicious oatmeal in Echo Park if they did not work so hard. What if we didn't have farmers? We would be pretty hungry, and life would be fucked up!

After the oats are harvested, they go to the factory for milling. I am grateful for the people who came up with, manufactured, and run the milling machines. At the factory, the tougher outer part of the oat gets taken off and is used for animal feed, and the soft inner part is baked in big ovens; gets cut into pieces, bagged up, and put into boxes; and finally, arrives in stores so we can enjoy it. I am thankful to YouTube, for all the knowledge about oatmeal I just gained.

That is a simple illustration, but do you see how gratitude will help you love everything around you. See how many people grow and create this oatmeal? I am grateful for all of them. Start looking at the simple things in your life and see the steps that were taken before it came into your life and now makes your life better. It takes an army of people to do things, who are often invisible. We forget to be grateful. Don't! Gratitude makes you love your present and appreciate the second chances you get in life so you can live a bullshit-free life. This is the only precious life we are given. Be generous with this superpower, because it makes life memorable. Here are some things I do that help me to let gratitude create magic in my life.

1. **Take a gratitude walk.** If you can do this every day. If not, at least once a week. On your walk, look around you calmly. What do you see? What do you hear? What do you smell? What do you taste? What do you touch? These kinds of walks are healing and grounding and will surprise you. You will see things that you have overlooked for many years.
2. **Make a gratitude advice list**. What advice have you received from people that dramatically changed the trajectory of your life? Then imagine, if you never met those people, how would your life be? Would you still be stuck doing things that made you unhappy? Make this list and reflect on it.
3. **Write a grateful email to an old friend or somebody who helped you big time in your life.** Go back in your old diaries, or your memories, or cards you received, and see who you forgot about. Tell them you were thinking about your

past and wanted to write them and tell them how thankful you are for them. Even after all those years, you have not forgotten about them. You make them and yourself smile. I thought about Mike the printer this morning. He has a print shop in Van Nuys. If you need magical printing, go visit him. Tell him I said hi.

4. **Notice one new thing per day.** Look around you and observe one thing you've never paid attention to daily, that you just take for granted, but that makes your life much easier. Imagine that that thing was not there anymore or was taken away from you. Sometimes little tiny things are beneficial to keep the world spinning. Just look at a little screw that holds up your bed. It held my body for years till the bed went crashing down recently. Notice the small things in life.

5. **Start a gratitude journal or incorporate gratitude in your diary writing.** Write down what you are grateful for and let it fill you up with happiness. There is so much we have, but we often focus on the things we lack.

6. **Smile at people.** Smiling feels good for you and the receiver. You will give them happiness and a little comfort. Smiling is contagious, too, so get going.

7. **See gratitude as a form of art.** You are the artist and your paint is the gratitude with which you create your environment. Use a lot of colors!

8. **Do the "What if?" exercise.** Ask yourself,

"What if I did not have a roof above my head?" "What if I did not have a job that lets me pay my bills?" "What if I did not have a car that takes me where I need to go?" "What if my best friend never called me?" "What if the strawberry I am about to eat was never grown?" "What if the sun did not shine anymore, or never came back?" "What if the surgeon never operated on my family member?" "What if the social worker never helped the orphan who needed help?" "What if my favorite writer never wrote that book that changed my life?" "What if I was never born?"

The "What-if?" exercise will give you more appreciation for many things you are taking for granted. Commit to practice gratitude often. You will live longer, better, and wiser.

CHAPTER 25:

POWER

HALF OF YOUR MASTERY OF POWER COMES FROM WHAT YOU DO NOT DO.
—Robert Greene

Be Yourself; Everyone Else Is Already Taken.
Oscar Wilde revealed a powerful statement: "Be yourself." People who own their personal power live authentic lives. They are brave, conquer their fears, follow their dreams, and help and inspire others. Some even help humanity progress and give hope and guidance along the way. We admire and look up to them.

It Makes the World Go Round

Power is the root of strength that keeps everything going. The power of a dam, the power of our collective energy, the power of the sun, the power of our heart, the power of our minds are all needed to keep society functioning. To reach the life you desire, you must have personal power. Personal power is all about the mastery of yourself: not controlling other people or wanting to control them. When you own personal power, you are self-aware and have vision and a positive outlook. You have a natural self-assertion and a healthy striving for love. And this makes you powerful.

Creating Personal Power

Personal power is the kind of power you create. It is the energy you send out and exchange with the people around you. Your personal power helps you to communicate effectively, which can help those around you. Nothing is more rewarding than improving lives because you conquered yourself first. Increasing your personal power can help you live a longer and happier life.

How to Get This Personal Power?

First know yourself. This means to discover yourself regularly. What do you do in certain situations? What do you let go of easily? Are you triggered by injustice? Are you a fighter? Do you look for peace most of the time? Delve into your psyche and commit to learning about yourself. When you get a sense of your authentic self, you won't be afraid to express what you think or feel. Then be bold. Timid souls get cowardly results. Let your power shine through brightly, and approach life with zest. Have courage and let your passion appear instead of damping it with insecurities. Let your authentic self flourish by acting, speaking, and living your life fully.

Get out of a victim state. Lots of us attribute our unhappiness to others. But others cannot have an influence, or control us, if we do not let them. Make your self-worth independent from other people.

Others can advise you, help you, and listen to you, but do not let others fully take over. Do not scrutinize your happiness because of what somebody else did to you. Stay strong in your own power and progress. Know your values; they will guide you.

Select the Right Emotions from Your Personal Jukebox

You need to master an important skill to own your power: controlling your emotions.

You can begin this process by regulating your breathing. When we are angry, for instance, our breathing becomes more rapid and uncontrolled. Rumi said, "The cure for the pain is in the pain." Instead of eating or drinking your pain away, let it pass through and do not judge it. When you judge your pain, you keep it in your system longer. Examine it to try to understand your feelings. Knowing yourself is key; self-awareness is the first step to personal power.

Emotions are beautiful, unless they hijack your life. Within the jukebox of emotions, pick the right song! Pay attention to them, and if an emotion is controlling you, try to figure out why. This will lead to understanding yourself, and the more you know, the more personal power you have.

Power Drainage
Be aware of things that tax your emotions. This can happen through intensive watching of news or TV, reading online gossip, or listening to negative people. Keep your valuable energy high so you can keep your power up. You do not want to become a deflated air mattress after you've listened to negative folks going into detail on why their lives suck so much. Especially when you have given them several suggestions, on several occasions, for how to change. When they still bombard you with the same broken-ass record, it is time for you to distance yourself.

Hang Out with People That Empower You
Life is too short, especially when we get into our later years. Hang out with people who empower and transfer some of their power to you. I always see it in their eyes. People who are powerful shine with special energy, and it's contagious!

They do not bullshit around. Surround yourself with people who want to see you grow, people who appreciate you and share their wisdom, so you can empower each other in good and bad times.

That Special Beam Is Passion
If you are able to do things with deep passion, you will get your power on. There is nothing as strong as passion. Passion can create miracles. It can bend steel. Passion makes the impossible, possible. Use your passion to help people. Do not use your passion to hurt

others. Do not be an opportunist. Treat people like you want to be treated. That is the most powerful thing to do. Let your passion shine and illuminate all the people around you. It empowers a universe!

Research Powerful People

Most people with personal power have integrity. They respect themselves. That is why Muhammad Ali said no to the war. He was not going to go, even when the government forced him to go. Even if it cost him part of his career, he did not allow injustice to happen and did not serve in the war. I admire him for that. He did, by the way, help free prisoners of a war later on! Thank you, Ali, for doing the right things. Get to know people with personal power and learn from them. They do not have to be celebrities. A random person can give you powerful advice. Be open to it.

Stop Worrying

Worrying depletes power massively. It leaves you drained, and it's often for nothing; we fill in the blanks with things that *might* happen in the future, but most of the time *do not* happen. We are often in a state of fear and feed ourselves with negative emotions. Place worry where it belongs, far away, and not in your mind, heart, or around you at all. Learn to eliminate worry from your life, and you will have clarity and peace. And if worry comes up, look at how you can change it into taking massive action.

Worry does not want you to live your kick-ass life. The most important thing I learned when I worry too much is to keep up with my good habits. They help me let go of my worries. Let it go and feel your power come back.

Most Develop Power Later in Life

Our life experiences give us power; our values develop through our reactions to events. Through experiencing life, we begin to know ourselves. This is a gift that aging brings. It is your privilege to claim your power. People who are powerful handle fear in a better way. Fear will never go away. We know by now that it comes down to what you do with fear. Will you run, or will you see yourself as a one-man army and fight?

The powerful fight and push through inconvenience and complacency. This isn't easy, and many of us don't choose that path because, let's be real here, many of us do not want to go into the unfamiliar. How many people have said, "I am going to do this or that," but they when found out they actually had to put some hard work in, work that could hurt, they gave up?

Don't let that be you. Do not give up! Ever! You have the opportunity to look back at experiences you wish had been different and learn from them. From experience comes wisdom, and from wisdom comes knowledge, and from knowledge comes power. You have a life-changing opportunity to act on the wisdom you've gained. Be strong so you will get to that powerful state too. What is the pain threshold you can handle, and can you go a little bit further next time? Remember that to grow, we have to get uncomfortable first. That is how athletes progress. Nobody is asking you to go from a person sitting on a couch to running a marathon in a week. Little by little, expand yourself. This is called *stretching*, and one day you will look back and say, did I really do that? I, who never got up because the bag of potato chips was too delicious and kept me stuck? Yes, you fucking did that, and you will do more if you can silence your excuses and become stronger. Make a start today, but be humble with your progress. It will not always go fast. Some of us have beginner's luck and things happen faster, but it never is what it looks like. Have patience with your mediocrity in the beginning, as you become better.

Next, I say something that might sound contrary.

Know When to Be Soft

In the Tao Te Ching, Lao Tzu says, "Water is fluid, soft, and yielding. But water will wear away rock, which is rigid and cannot yield. As a rule, whatever is fluid, soft, and yielding will overcome whatever is rigid and hard. This is another paradox: what is soft is strong."

You have probably heard the fable of the Oak and the Willow, where the unbending, strong oak tree was broken by the powerful wind, but the flexible willow tree just swayed in the wind. Powerful people know that when you are hard, you are always pushing against the forces coming against you, and eventually you will wear out and break. But to be truly strong, one needs to know how to be soft and flexible, so they can keep going. Life ebbs and flows, and if you resist this natural phenomenon, you get friction. You cannot always be powerful. You have to rest to get your power back and also give space to others. Allow others to also win in the arena. Know when you need to share.

Embrace the Difficult Things

My biggest power boosts came when I finally took care of all the difficult things in my life: my finances, exercising, food, my family, my living situation, and becoming crystal clear on what I wanted in life. If you face your issues, your power will expand. I did not sweep my excuses under a carpet anymore; I dealt with my issues one by one in a calm and focused way.

If I can do it, so can you! Never give up. This will make you powerful.

CHAPTER 26:
RESOURCEFULNESS

> **NOW IS NO TIME TO THINK OF WHAT YOU DO NOT HAVE.
> THINK OF WHAT YOU CAN DO WITH WHAT THERE IS.**
> —Ernest Hemingway

If it weren't for resourcefulness, I would not be living in Los Angeles. I always wanted to study in the United States but did not have the financial capital for it. I had the tenacity for working a full-time job, going to school in the evenings, and taking acting classes on the weekends, but I also had a huge loan, and not much room to come up with $30,000 for studying in the United States for a year.

I realized that if I wanted to make my dream a reality I had to do something completely different. My biggest expense was my rent. Somebody I knew had a super tiny empty room in their attic that was used as a storage place. I asked if I could sleep there so I could sublet my place. For months I slept in a spot where when you turned to your left, you would hit a wall, and when you turned to your right, you'd hit another wall. There was no space at all, but it did not matter. I was happy because in the meantime I rented out my place to an expat and saved the money. My bank account grew enough to pay tuition for a private acting school, but it was still going too slow. I needed more cash to live in the States.

Then a lucky star shone upon me. The bank where I worked was going to reorganize two years after I planned to quit. I would leave and get zero money for working there for ten years. When they reorganized, people would be asked to leave, or stay if there still was a suitable job for them after reorganization. It was a voluntary way of leaving the bank. Cash dispensers had replaced many jobs, so the bank needed less manpower. I already was delayed by a year on moving to Hollywood and did not want to wait two more years. Then a friend of mine and I thought about making the impossible, possible. What if we asked the bank to give me money now instead of waiting till the reorganization happened in two years? At that point I did not even know if they would offer me this "let go fee" two years later. Because of my employment history I would probably be asked to stay. I would not be offered severance pay. But I wanted out and also to get some money that would help me move to Los Angeles.

If It Sounds Crazy, Then Go for It

It was a crazy idea, because technically they did not have to pay me anything. We discussed our plan intensively. We convinced the bank to offer the severance pay to me now. This had never been done before. Why would a bank give money to somebody who already wanted to leave? My luck was that for all the years I worked there, I was consistent in delivering excellent work and worked hard. I excelled in my duties. I saw the bank people as my family! I made them lots of money. My reviews were excellent, and my bosses loved my dedication. So due to my great track record and the bank director convincing his boss in the main office, I was able to get ten months of salary. Now I could go to the United States and finally start on this crazy, beautiful dream I had: to become an actress in Hollywood.

> Resourcefulness is the key to lasting success!

They Get It Done

Resourceful people get more done than others. They find ways to create magic where others throw in the towel. Resourcefulness is the ability to find quick and clever ways to overcome difficulties. A resourceful person is like a magician; he or she will pull tricks out of a hat. Try to cultivate this superpower when possible. Sometimes we think we do not have a way to get out of a situation, but there is always a way. If there is no open door in front of you, then create your own door. Build it, draw it, stampede through it, but do something. By taking action your resource-infused power will shine. Be creative and invent a way out. The key is to switch things up sometimes. Look at things in a different way. How could you become more resourceful?

Work with What You Have

What are your resources now? For me it was my friend, who is a brilliant consultant and previously negotiated contracts with companies. I would never have been able to do the talks with the bank without my friend. One way to determine this is to first look around you at who you know. Make a list and do not hesitate to go back in the past or even decades ago. If you were nice to people in the past, they would remember you and often put effort in to help you. Do you know a lawyer friend who could help you with a contract for a friend's price or even do it for free if you take him out for lunch? Hey, lawyers need to eat too, right? Do you know a restaurant owner who could let you use his space to hold an event when he's less busy? Do you know a professor who could write you a recommendation letter for a job? Do you have a friend who works in a company that you can reach out to for a sponsorship? Look around and leverage your network.

Be Open-Minded

Manage to keep the right mindset to allow solutions to come to you. Do not get discouraged or give up. Always listen to good old Winston Churchill's advice here, "Never, never, never [never] give up." I added an extra "never" in there just to make it hit home. When you are open-minded, you will be able to turn problems into solutions. Where others stop because they think something is not possible, you still go and still search, and you will find something that will help you. By staying open-minded, you will be able to adapt better in difficult situations.

Switch Solutions Upside Down
If you thought A then think M instead. Come up with solutions that initially sound crazy. Crazy is only crazy till it is done. Then it becomes brilliant in the eyes of the non-resourceful people.

Be Super Confident
Stretch what you think is possible. You do that by cultivating confidence. Know deep inside that whatever happens, a solution will appear. Have that as a goal. Edison said he did not fail ten thousand times; it just took him ten thousand tries to get it right. It took him time to invent the light bulb, but he was patient and confident that he would eventually get it done. Get it done—just like Edison!

Have Sacred Deadlines
Tell yourself to come up with something by a certain date. When there is a deadline, it becomes a necessity, and you become more creative and do not waste time.

Paired with persistence, this will create wonderful

ideas, not always the best ones immediately, but that does not matter. You are working hard and brainstorming to find your eureka moment. You will be able to do more with less because of the power of resourcefulness.

Become a Detective

How would a detective approach this? A detective understands everyone's interest in the current situation. What does the other party want? What do you want, and how can you create a win-win situation for all parties involved? Sometimes it is not money that will give the right outcome. Recall stories such as the Trojan horse or the classic fairytale of "Jack and the Beanstalk," where Jack trades a cow for a handful of beans. Resourcefulness always works and is a valuable skill to cultivate. Start living your dreams sooner by integrating resourcefulness.

Never Give Up

Resourceful people do not give up. They keep going because they know that within the maze of life, they will find a way out and kick ass. They will find the right paths that lead them to their sweet dreams. They know that dedication sprinkled with the power of resourcefulness will get them where they want to be.

CHAPTER 27:

CONSISTENCY OF HABITS

> **WE ARE WHAT WE REPEATEDLY DO. EXCELLENCE, THEN, IS NOT AN ACT, BUT A HABIT.**
> —Aristotle

It never fails, anytime there is a long line at the women's restroom, there's one woman that goes in and takes her time while the others wait outside. I mean, she really takes her T-I-M-E in there. I always joke that there should be a TV screen hanging inside the toilet stall to show the person inside doing their business that people are waiting outside, so they will hurry up.

The women in line think, "Can't this chick hurry up a bit? Our bladders are at war with us." At last the woman in the toilet comes out, looking relieved, and another woman goes in, again taking way too long.

Enter me: I go into the restroom, and a few seconds later, I jump out. Every woman in line looks at me in disbelief, like I am a ghost or something. I would see the expressions on their faces: "Is this really true? Is she fucking done already with peeing or whatever shit she was doing inside? How is this possible? She just went in!"

I used to have a habit of doing everything fast in life, from going into toilets, to eating, to thinking, to living my life. It wasn't till I started the habit of slowing down that I saw how much I was missing. I flew through life like I was on one of those fast trains in Japan, full speed, rushing because Tokyo was waiting. When I started to slow down and indulge more in the present moment, and I mean deliberately slow down, I would start seeing details I was blind to before.

Slow down to live more in the present. Slowing down is key, and this new habit gave me a springboard to feeling better and making effective changes.

Be Consistent with Your Habits

I wish somebody had dragged me by my hair, kicked my butt, or told me in another effective way how *super important* it was to be consistent with your habits.

The moment your chosen habits become automatic, and they do not receive extra thought, you just do them, like brushing your teeth, or washing your face, is the moment when you finally start seeing success. Before I knew this important wisdom, I only did certain habits based on the whims of my emotions. If I felt like it or felt "inspired," I would write, exercise, eat healthier, stop overthinking, and apply other habits that make life worthy. It should not matter. If the sun is shining, rain is pouring, hurricanes are raging, a blizzard is blowing, an earthquake is shaking, or whatever other force is trying to inhibit you, certain habits should be done with consistency. That is how you get rid of your bullshit and kick major ass in your life.

The Right Habits Bring Freedom and Growth

One of my favorite quotes is, "We are what we repeatedly do. Excellence, then, is not an act, but a habit." We have to be consistent with the good habits we choose. If there is no consistency, then there is no growth. I recently learned a lot from *The Power of Habits* by Charles Duhigg, especially the first part where the author describes the so-called *habit loop* with the mouse. I realized I was acting like that little mouse. In his book Charles explains how habits form in our brains. He writes about the process by which a practice becomes a habit. The habit loop consists of three parts: a *cue*, a *routine*, and a *reward*. A cue is your trigger and tells your brain to go into an automatic mode. It then selects the appropriate habit. Let's say it is 3:00 p.m. and you see advertising about chocolate. You crave this chocolate because it is the end of your working day and you feel tired, so you run to the vending machine to buy some milk chocolate with nuts. The activity you perform after your cue is your routine. It is how you satisfy your craving. Your reward is more energy. You think your reward is the chocolate, but what you want is what this chocolate can do for you—make you less tired.

Cravings are at the center of these habit loops.

They keep habit loops going, and when they become automatic, they transform into habits. The important lesson is to keep the cue and the reward but change your routine. Choose other routines and get a reward that is better for you. Let's say you still get the cue at 3:00 p.m., feeling tired, but you think first and realize what you want is an energy boost, not necessarily the calorie-rich chocolate. Instead of the chocolate, you buy or make a smoothie. It is much healthier and still satisfies your cravings. The smoothie gives you a satisfying reward by making you feel more energetic. Try replacing the kinds of rewards you give yourself. Here are other things I implemented in my life to get better habits and to keep them.

Make a Master List for the Year with Your Goals and Hang It on Your Wall

Have one master list you work with during the year. Include your important goals of what you want to accomplish. I have mine above my desk, so when I write or sit at my desk, I always see it. I let it marinate into my subconsciousness. Write this handwritten list on your birthday or on January 1. Both days will give you the excitement you need to come up with great goals to pursue. During the year, look at what goals you did not reach yet and ask yourself *why* you did not accomplish them. This is powerful and will help you either to achieve them in the upcoming year or change something in your current behavior that will allow you to reach them still.

Mini List for What to Do the Next Day

Make a mini list and write this every night before going to bed. Have mini goals for the next day ready to take on. When you get up in the morning, do not run around like a headless chicken. Just finish your list. Those two lists have bettered my life. Now my days are filled with important and concrete things. I feel pre-excitement that works into my sleep cycle the night before when I jot it down. I write down things like: "Write at least 1,000 words," "Reach out to my editor," and other things I should not forget to do. Every time you delete one of the items on the list, you will feel additional excitement that motivates you to keep going. It is like a good drug.

Create Habits That You Can Follow

Do not put too many things on your daily list. Otherwise you will get overwhelmed. You don't need that. You might overextend yourself and not do any of them. Sometimes we want too much too fast, like going to the gym the first day and wanting to exercise for three hours. Do not do that to yourself. Build up wisely so you can keep doing your new habits.

Emotion Control

I made an effort to control my emotions more. Instead of letting them all come out like bursts of thunder, I let them be more like the little lights in a candle. What helped me tremendously with emotion control was studying the Stoics. The Stoics from Greece found out how to live more rationally. A great book to read on this topic is *Meditations* by Marcus Aurelius, which I mentioned earlier in the book. If we make a habit not to let emotions come out uncontrollably, we gain a lot in life.

Put Things in Perspective

Is this nasty woman at the cash register really worth dwelling on for forever? Is my coworker who asks me an unfair request worth dwelling on? Is the car in front of me that is moving slower than a bicycle worth tensing up my muscles and having my heartbeat go through the car's roof? No, it is not worth it. Learn how to think more in terms of, "Everything is good the way it is." It is life, and life is not always perfect. What keeps me in perspective is to not sweat the small stuff and to always remind myself that people are suffering in other countries or even down the street.

Being Nice and Sweet to the Body

It wasn't till I got injuries that I realized how much I took this temple we are given for granted. I just did not see how special my body was. I've got legs, sure. "Run faster," I thought. I've got arms. "Sure, push them harder," I said to myself. I've got ears. "Sure, hear more and get annoyed at neighbors chatting late at night." Our body is a magical machine that has given us power to an unlimited extent. Do not always use your body to the maximum. Give it some breaks from time to time. Give it a nice massage, talk nicely to your hurt knee, and stroke your neck with gentle touches. Be nice to your body so it will be nicer to you. Give it days off. This new habit improved my life.

Stop Being a Maximizer

I used to be a maximizer, or a perfectionist as it is more commonly known. If a situation was not perfect, I would not start. "Oh, that situation is not happening yet. I will just wait." Waiting is deadly because it kills dreams softly. Looking for the most perfect thing out there delays your progress. Many times, during trips with my friends, I would not eat at a restaurant close to us. I studied restaurants with rave reviews and wanted to check out those places, even if it meant walking for an hour to the other side of town with a hungry friend next to me. My friends were usually very patient because they know me. Now I give into more spontaneous eating. I choose something *good enough* instead of always waiting for the best.

Now, don't get me wrong, I am talking about simple daily things here. For certain things, the bigger goals, you still must go for the best in your life. But the day-to-day things can be simple. It'll make your life easier.

The Habit of Creating Forget-About-What-Time-It-Is-Now Chunks

When you stop being a slave of time, you will make time to create more magic. Take your watch off, put your phone away, and just float in time without thinking about it much. This can be liberating. Just sit and dream without the clock ticking. The constant obsession with time can take a lot of our creativity away. Implement a habit of sometimes just forgetting about time. Just be and let the magic happen.

Saving Money

Boy has this been an important new habit. If it wasn't for saving money, I would not have been able to create a chunk of free time for myself to write a first draft for this book in a few months! I saved money by cutting out buying the unnecessary stuff. Even if you start with just a few bucks, make a habit of saving. It grows faster than you think. You can start today. Also implement days where you do not spend one penny. It empowers.

The Art of the Start

Starting is smart; finishing is divine. Realize again how super lucky you are to be living and able to go after the dreams of your heart. Have patience with your current situation and realize that so many other people, and we are talking millions here, wish they had just 1 percent of what you have. Do not create the habit of taking things for granted. Nothing is permanent, and everything can be taken away from you in a split second.

A Bad Day Is Okay

If you have a bad day and fall into your temptation, then do not beat yourself up. It happens. C'est la vie. We are human. Be a sinner for a day, and the next day go back to consistency and keep those habits you worked so hard to accomplish.

Keep habits as long as they work, but be open to changing them if they stop working for you.

Know what you have, and thank your lucky stars often. Patience is key for turning something meaningful into a habit. You will impress people if you accomplish new habits and stick to them. You will inspire others to take some of these habits on themselves. I had a friend who started running after she cheered me on at the marathon I ran in Paris.

CHAPTER 28:

POSITIVE MINDSET

THE POSITIVE THINKER SEES THE INVISIBLE, FEELS THE INTANGIBLE, AND ACHIEVES THE IMPOSSIBLE.
—Winston Churchill

People with a positive mindset are happier, get more done, change the world, are healthier, and believe in something bigger than themselves. A positive attitude is your life preserver when you are about to drown in this ocean called life. Having a positive mindset has saved me several times. When I lost hope, I increased my positive thoughts and saved myself. When I was in pain, I let positivity fill me up and heal me.

> Time, thinking positively, and love are the top three cures.

Your Life Vest in Stormy Waters

When I almost gave up, I strengthened my positive mindset and was able to stay strong. It helps in unimaginable ways. It keeps you going, in moments of pure darkness. It creates a path to walk on and get your power back.

I had one of my darkest periods when I was fifteen. I had my midlife crisis early. (I told you I am always fast with everything I do.) Life was full of pain, and I did not see the light anymore. I desperately wanted to become my own self but could not because I was surrounded by overly strict parents who did not give me space to breathe or live the life I desired. I reached deep inside myself, pulled all my power out through the help of positive thinking and a positive mindset, and found the solution.

I decided to run away from home. I knew a life without them would save my life. I ran away and lived for years in teenage runaway shelters. Those were some of the best years of my life because I was finally free. A positive mindset gave me this power and still does.

Stop the Cynical Beast Taking Over

Many people become cynical when things do not go the way they want them to go. They look at things with darkness and gloom. But why? I ask. Why not change it into something better? If I remain home, overeat, treat my body harshly, and think negative thoughts, how can change occur in my life? It will not! The cynical beast has to find himself another buddy. Kick him out of your house.

Fill Yourself with Your Light

Change happens when we fill ourselves with our divine light, the light we turn on brightly by staying positive, the light we follow so hopefully, we never give up. Let our divine lights meet each other so we can change the world. We believe in something bigger. We are the dreamers; we are the risk-takers. Positive thinking literally fills you up with divinity and makes you stronger. I feel it when I am at home and fill myself up with it generously. It flows through my heart, my cells, blood, my whole being and warms me up. Like a little flower, it grows inside me and makes me stronger. Positivity lets me flourish and create beauty. Think about this deeply. And if you are still thinking, "I'm not sure about this rosy-colored positive thinking," then what is the alternative?

By staying negative, you will never change your current situation. If this is what you want, nobody can stop you, but let me tell you, what a waste it would be for your life. What a disaster it would be if you were not able to find your place on this earth. Give it at least a try. Do not think that life has given up on you. Stay positive and move forward big time! But remember that being positive does not mean you do not get to work hard on your goals. Thinking only positive thoughts is not fucking enough to get rid of all the bullshit. Think positive thoughts and then act. Big time!

Positive Thinking Gives Hope

When you temporarily lose hope, positive thoughts reveal clarity. A positive mindset helps you imagine better times when you had hope in your life. Instill this magical power and do not listen to the naysayers or people that try to make you feel bad. They love the word no. They want to stay negative because they do not want to grow, become better, contribute, change the world, develop, and give big. How do you think positively?

Imagine Better Times to Come

See how your future will be better when you take action. Your imagination will guide you and let you see what life can be in better times. See it clearly and delve deep into the details. See it in your mind's eye. Practice often so you can do it in real life.

Stay Away from Negative People

Stay away from negative people like the plague. Negative people suck positivity away, and that is not what you want. You want a positive mindset to help you reach the unimaginable. It is hard to maintain the necessary positivity with negative people in your life. If you find it hard to stay away from negative people you care about, you can tell them you are too busy to spend time with them, tell them you have to leave when they start to become negative, or tell them to be more positive! It will help you limit your exposure to them, and it could help them change their ways. Either way, say these things with a smile so they do not land as hard.

Observe Others Who Have It Worse

When I feel sorry for myself, I remind myself that many have it worse. This puts things into perspective. Millions have no food, no love, no house, no money, no kindness, and no bright future. I remind negative people to look at others who have it worse than them. Sometimes they reevaluate and change. If we are positive, we can help instead of letting others suffer. Cherish your positivity and keep going. Positivity makes your life easier, while negativity keeps you living a bullshit life.

Train Your Mind to Remain Positive

First, observe your negative thoughts. We have thousands of negative thoughts daily. Usually a few come to the surface and are dominant. Let's start with a thought I feel come up often: "I feel fat today. My stomach is as big as a spaceship." When I think this, I might decide not to go out and to stay home instead. My first step when I start thinking negatively is to observe my current situation for what it is. Then I find my "but."

Find Your "But"

My second step is to add the word "but" to it. "My stomach is big, *but* I am working on getting it flatter by running." "My stomach is big, *but* by staying home, I will only feel sorrier for myself. I need to get the hell out and live this beautiful life." "My stomach is big, *but* by locking myself up, I will not enjoy the beautiful sun outside." Add the word *but* to negative thoughts and rewire your brain back to positivity.

Let us experience our present and future brightly! Stay positive so you can finally change your life. Stay positive so you can live a life that many others dream of. Be positive so you can change yourself and help the world by setting an example. You can do this, and you will.

CHAPTER 29:

LOVE

HE WHO LOVES, FLIES, RUNS, AND REJOICES; HE IS FREE, AND NOTHING HOLDS HIM BACK.
—Henri Matisse

How can something so important be invisible? If it were an object, people with bad intentions could pick love up and steal it. If it were tangible, tyrants could kill it. Why is a poem often about love? Why are songs about love? Why are there so many movies about love? Why are some of our favorite books about love?

> Dear love, you show up everywhere, because you are everything.

Love is everything worth living for. It is our oxygen. It is our blood. It is our light. We share our love because it is the master power of all superpowers. It is the big enabler in life. Love arises beyond the mind. Through love, you awaken. Finally, you see the world how it is supposed to be seen. A magical, giving, calming, kind force that makes challenges and pain fall into nothingness. Love is Providence. Let love empower you to live your best life!

Start with the Most Important Love First—Self-Love

The love you give yourself is the most important, because you deserve it. You are a special person. Even with almost eight billion people on our planet, there is nobody else like you. Just how you were made was a miracle. Have you ever thought about this on a deeper level? What were the chances of you being born? Hundreds of coincidences happened before you came to this world. Feel your specialness. Feel that you matter and deserve to give and receive love. If your heart is not filled with love, you might have success, but it will be temporary. Life immersed in love is divine. It moves previously unmovable mountains. Let this power guide and empower you.

Love Is a Spiritual Practice

Sometimes love is easy, and sometimes it is very messy and hard. We all feel enchanted by the cute puppy, our heart warms up, and we give it love while the owner walks by, but can we give love to our parents who have mistreated us? Can we give love to the beggar on the street with his dirty, smelly clothes? Can we give love to people who have acted with no tact? Can we give love to the busy restaurant owner when he brings us the wrong dish on one of the busiest days of the year at his restaurant?

Love Needs to Be Worked On

It does not always happen automatically. We have to show our love to others like there is no tomorrow. Heal your hurt heart by giving more love. Mark Twain said, "The best way to cheer yourself up is to try to cheer somebody else up." The fastest way to feel better is to love others and mean it.

> We are in a love drought, and it is the reason why humanity feels ill.

How can you love more?

Increase Your Love for Others

Show your love to others in small ways, because that is what matters most, the sweet little details you do with care. It is that special text you wrote, it is that special phone call you made, it is that special surprise appearance you made, it is that listening ear you gave, it is offering to pick them up from the airport. It is the encouragement you gave before your friend went to that important job interview. It is that flower bouquet you sent when your friend bought her first house. It is the cake you baked when your friend got engaged. Show your love and spread its power and magic.

Do Things That Make You Happy
Find your purpose in life, and then work hard to pursue it. There is only one life. Do not waste it by doing things that make you unhappy. Instead, fill your heart and mind up by living your purpose. Do things that make you happy, so you will feel the love inside and can spread it to others. This is the only way you will get love in return.

> Time not spent on love, is time wasted. Some of us took a few extra years, to get to where we are. Commit to living a brilliant life by loving more.
>
> Do things with love, so time will not be robbed from you anymore.

Love is the superpower we have in our hearts and minds. Nobody was born without love. It is the great equalizer.

Pay Attention to Faces
There is love in faces. Take them in. Let the energy of a friend's face enchant you. Take a moment the next time you meet somebody to observe their face and take it all in. Take it in fully. See their eyes, how do they look? Are they in pain? Are they in love? Are they full of questions? How can you help them with some of their dreams?

I am not talking about doing this with the creepy guy or girl who wants to ask you on a date when you are not interested. No need to observe them; you will send the wrong message. I am talking about people who you care about or that you meet in random encounters. Really see them next time!

Random encounters can be super powerful. So many times I have changed my perspective in life because of advice I received from somebody I just met.

> Do not look with dead eyes. Look with attention. Next time you meet a friendly face, observe it, look deeper, and get a glimpse of someone's soul.

Nature Is a Giant Lover

Our greatest lover is around us every day. I wrote a whole chapter about nature, I love nature so much. Going into nature will let you love more. Nature is often all you need. Soak in the fresh air, let the sunshine sprinkle you with her abundance, feel the wind play with your hair, observe the tallness of trees, and appreciate the work nature does to keep us alive.

> Go into nature to become you.

Love Your Body

Love your body by appreciating all that it does. Your body is a love machine. I had two accidents that made me pause the rush button of life and go deeper into my appreciation of my body. It all could have been worse, but my body saved me. It fought hard so I could recover faster.

Check up on your body. How does it feel? What does it need that you are not giving it? It is very important to do this regularly. When I had my knee injury during my running sessions, I realized how extremely important my knees were. I had never given love to my knees before. "What baloney," I thought, "Loving your knees!" But now, let me tell you that I have changed dramatically. My knees are my champions. I adore them! Because of my knees I am mobile. Because of my knees my lovely body can walk. I massage my knees now. I give them love and appreciate them because I felt how it was to live without them functioning properly. I was in pain! I gave them rest during my injury, by sleeping longer hours and not walking more than needed.

Besides the knees, there is our heart. How is your heart feeling? Have you given love to your heart lately? Have you thanked it for fucking beating for you every day? Day in and day out, it works hard without getting paid. Pay it by giving it more love. Maybe go do that art project that makes your heart happy. Touch your heart and express your gratitude for it showing up every day and doing the work. Do it right now!

Touch your heart now and say, thank you heart!

Have you thought about your intestines working nonstop every day without complaining? Just the bladder is doing a superhuman job. We are so lucky with our body. Give it love nonstop! Let love explode inside of you and heal it from the inside.

Make Lovely Things

Make something with love. There is love in making that perfect cake. There is love when you take that first bite from it too—or more bites, like I would do. Create that cake and eat it up like it is your last motherfucking day on earth. Come up with a new recipe, so good that it fills up your senses with joyfulness. Start a new painting and feel love explode inside through the lovely colors you are using. Draw a silly picture, laugh about it, and share it to spread love. Making things with love is special. Create more and feel more love. The making will fill your body with love and nurture you. Make something lovely.

Love Is Messy!

We are hurt birds but do not always show it. We tell ourselves that we are strong and have no pain. The reason we are jealous, envious, restless, and carry negative emotions around is because in the past we were hurt instead of loved. You might be mad at somebody, but sometimes being right should make room for being loved. Reach out to that person, especially if the pain is eating you alive. If you think you will feel more peace by letting them go, then that is another story, but if they are important to you, please reach out. Forgive and give yourself love in exchange. Do not see it as if you are giving in, like you are weak. See it as being smart, for your heart, for your progress, and to not to add more pain to your present, caused by your past. Release yourself and feel love coming back into your body. This will not always be easy but is often needed.

Do Not Let Past Hurt Stop You

We are too stingy with our love because our little hearts got hurt, and therefore we are cautious because we do not want to be hurt again. But what is love without hurt? We would never know what love was if we did not experience hurt. Do not close yourself off. That is the worst thing you can do. Help heal the pain of our universe. Give love to strangers, friends, family, friends-to-become, coworkers, everybody who is around. People need it. Now more than ever! Many of us are in pain and are not showing it.

Be Open

Be open and you gain more. Do not close yourself off like a thick, inflexible wall. Be the door in that wall and open yourself to magic. Recently I was riding the subway and a woman sat across from me and wanted to chat. I initially was hesitant to have a conversation, but I answered her question of how I was doing by also asking her how she was doing. She then said she was not doing well. She said she had two full-time jobs and that one of them made her unhappy because of a micromanager around. I told her she should make it a priority to look for another job. She then asked me what I did, and I said I write books. She replied: "You should write a book about me and my son." My eyes opened and my ears listened in because I was curious. She told me how her son became mute at the age of fifteen. He did not talk for years. She had an extremely hard time, working two jobs for a total of eighty hours a week, being a single mom, and now having a mute son. She rushed from one hospital to another to help her son speak again while having little extra time. He was now twenty-one and recently started speaking again.

She was happy, and her face lit up. I gave her space to talk, and when I left I saw her previous sadness transform into hope. She thanked me for listening, and I thanked her for sharing her story. By not cutting myself off, I had given her love, and it warmed my soul too. It was a special encounter with a stranger. Be open to others; you never know who you will help.

Don't Be Too Strict to Yourself or Others

If you want to love yourself more, give yourself some slack once in a while. Being too hard on yourself all the time works in a demotivating way. Look at how much you've already accomplished in your life. You are doing it, so give yourself a break. There is a time for everything. Sometimes we need pure discipline to move us forward, but sometimes we also need to loosen up those tightened elastics in life. Give yourself breathing room. Do not let strictness overwhelm you and take away joy. You should still enjoy things and keep discipline around in the right dosage.

Hang Out with Loving People

Hang around with people who shine love on others no matter where they are. They walk into a room and light it up.

> Hang out with the light shiners more often.

Light shiners are contagious and will make you feel happier. Wish the loveless people in your life good luck. Bless them with peace but move on.

> Know who not to get your love from.

We as humans have the possibility to transform lives. We can go beyond what we think is possible. Because love is lacking, we see decay. We see pain. We see frustration. We see bullying. We see crime. We see injustice. We see homelessness. Let us all take a little responsibility to fill up this void of pain and help the world heal.

> We crave love. We need it. But it starts with *you*.

Do not put this important emotion of love in the hands of others. You are the starter. You are the magician and creator of love. Open your heart more. Be spontaneous, forgive, listen, give, and believe you deserve love and that your love is wanted.

CHAPTER 30:

WHY NOT?

Why not? I am asking you to let these words sink deep into your heart.

Why not have the best life possible and with grace make your dreams a reality? Why not commit to give up on all your excuses once and for all, and go for it 100 percent?

....
We need people who are on fire.
....

We need people who are brave enough to make dreams come true. They make themselves happy and in the process, make others happy too. We need people who decide to go for it no matter what. We need you to step forward and claim your spot in the universe. We need you to unlock your greatness and share it widely! We need you to show others that a kick-ass life can be achieved.

....
"Why not?"—these two little words put together create dynamite!
....

Why not go after your wildest dreams? Why not let go of a job that makes you unhappy? Why not create a mindset of abundance? Why not do what *you* want? Why not move to another country? Why not start that exciting new company?

Why not finish writing that book?

Why not do what you have been putting off for many years?

"Why Not?" I Ask You Again!

Ask yourself what your "why nots?" in life are and change them into "I did thems."

Maybe you delayed yourself, because deep inside, you did not believe in yourself yet. You thought you could not do it, that you were not ready yet, that you were inadequate, but you are ready and you are more than adequate.

....
You are brave and ready!
....

I hope I have given you helpful insights on how to go for it. You've finished reading this book, and if you decide to change, I believe you will experience growth. Get rid of all the bullshit holding you back. I went through all this myself and experienced massive growth in my life. My life is now filled with purpose and happiness because I am doing what I love doing. Let me tell you that if a little girl, born in Africa, with no connections, shy, with little confidence when she was younger could turn herself around, then you can do this too. The gods are asking you to step forward and claim that place in the world that has not been filled yet.

> There is a void in the world, and only you can go in there and fill it up.

What would happen if you went for it? You'd help yourself, your friends, your family, your city, your state, your country, your continent, the world, and the universe.

The universe needs awakened people. So get up, face the world, dust yourself off, play a Diana Ross song, sing out loud, dance, and commit to that first step today. That first step will become a treasure chest to be shared with others in years to come.

Your contribution to humanity will save many people and create smiles on people's faces. A smile is the gold we carry on our face, so carry your smile with pride, because you went for it. You did it, you became a member of the awakened doers, and you finally found your home. It does not matter if everybody else is so-called killing it out there on social media. Stop looking at the outside for remedies.

> Focus on you.
> Focus on what you love doing.
> Focus on creating value for others.
> Pour all your heart and wisdom into it
> and share it with us.

You owe it to your heart to make your dreams a reality. Forget about jealousy, impatience, and despair. Focus on what you love doing and become wiser every single day. Work on everything that irritates you in life and get rid of it.

> Don't waste valuable life breaths anymore!

Have a gratefulness bonanza and cherish the unknown and heal thyself. I realized how extremely important it is to do work that I love. When I create inspiring writings, I change people's lives for the better. I help them find their destiny. When one does the work they love, they are on fire. They shine out truth and find their special place in life.

....

There is a void in the world. A void that only one person can fill. A person who found their destiny will claim that void and fill it up with their love, and the void will be gone. As a result, less pain will roam around in the world. The world will heal a little during this person's life. Their love will stay in the here and after.

....

Who Will You Become?

Who will you change into after you take all the steps, and face your fears, and totally go for it? What will your thoughts be? Who are the people you will be hanging out with? Who will you be helping? The new you is ready to burst into life with an enthusiasm not seen before. You will worry less about money, because it is coming to you easily now. You will work with passion as your compass now. You will pour all your love into your work, because you know it helps others. You are brave now!

....

Helping others is what it is about in life.
We are not lonely riders on this planet.

....

Live a Meaningful Life

Life is meaningful if we help people who are not as fortunate as us.

People who have received the lucky cards in their lives should help others and make others' lives a bit easier. The new you will be able to help others fulfill their dreams.

Imagine giving a big check to one of your best friends who has been struggling for years. See the tears on her face form when she looks at the check and then back at you full of gratitude. You have given her hope. You have given her a Band-Aid for all the pain she has been experiencing up till now.

> Hope is what needs to be sprinkled generously on people so they get empowered.

Be a Hope Creator

Have a fearless mind. How will it feel to go back to your old neighborhood, talk to people, and inspire them? How will it feel to build a teenage runaway shelter for the kids who were not dealt lucky cards regarding family? You can show them that things will be fine. They will find their destiny when the right time arrives. Sprinkle hope like an angel with a magic stick. How will you be able to help your family? Whether you have a good or bad relationship with your family, you can still help them. And do not forget strangers. I always say strangers are friends till proven wrong.

Marcus Aurelius said: *"Remember how long you've been putting this off, how many extensions the gods gave you, and you didn't use them. At some point you have to recognize what world it is that you belong to; what power rules it and from what source you spring; that there is a limit to the time assigned to you, and if you don't use it to free yourself it will be gone and will never return."*

Go for It, Thrive, Kick Ass, Become You

Find that place in the universe that needs to be filled with something only you can do. I will be cheering for you from my rocking chair sitting in the sun, smiling. My eighty-year-old-self will tell your eighty-year-old-self: "You are just getting started, kiddo."

ACKNOWLEDGMENTS

First, I would like to thank all my readers. I hope this book gives you the tools to get rid of your bullshit and kick ass! You deserve it. I put all my faith in you. Keep moving forward. Keep creating. Keep finding solutions, and keep believing that you, too, can accomplish that dream life you envision. Life is not always fair, but listen to your heart, develop your heart, and never, never, never, never give up. I want to thank my editor Lorraine Martindale. The moment I saw your name when searching for an editor, I knew I had to work with you. I want to thank my second editor, Ashleigh Bilodeau. You are a master in line editing and were able to give me additional nuggets of wisdom. I want to thank my third editor, Grammargal on Fiverr. Your editing skills are outstanding. You gave me fantastic insights. I want to thank my dear friend and sister Esther Dam. You were the first to read my book in the early stages. I remember the day after I ran the Paris Marathon, and you came to support me, how you delved into the first chapters. You read with enthusiasm and could not wait for it to be finished. You gave me hope, the hope I needed to keep going and publish this book, so I can help other people. I want to thank my dear friend and sister Helene Duetz. You were a phenomenal beta reader and helped me with line editing. Your insights made the book better. I see a new career for you in the near future! I want to thank my friend Jennifer Kelly. Your encouragement and suggestions were vital in bringing this book out. Your feedback on the book cover was appreciated. There are so many others I want to thank, but the list would be too long. I will save it for when we meet and drink a glass of champagne and cheer on this beautiful life we get to live. Thank you all for reading my book. Keep kicking major ass in your lives! You inspire me every day and allow me to live my purpose. Go get 'em, kiddo!

www.ingramcontent.com/pod-product-compliance
Lightning Source LLC
Chambersburg PA
CBHW031059080526
44587CB00011B/740